THE LIBRARY OF HOLOCAUST TESTIMONIES

An End to Childhood

An End to Childhood

MIRIAM AKAVIA

Translated from the Hebrew by
Michael P. McLeary and
Jeanette Goldman

With a Foreword by
ELIE WIESEL

VALLENTINE MITCHELL
LONDON • PORTLAND, OR

First published in 1995 in Great Britain by
VALLENTINE MITCHELL
Crown House, 47 Chase Side
Southgate, London N14 5BP

and in the United States of America by
VALLENTINE MITCHELL
c/o ISBS, 920 NE 58th Avenue, # 300
Portland, OR, 97213-3786

Website: http://www.vmbooks.com

First published in Hebrew © Miriam Akavia 1975
English translation copyright © 1995, 2003 Michael P. McLeary and Jeanette
Goldman

British Library Cataloguing in Publication Data

Akavia, Miriam
    An End to Childhood. (Library of Holocaust Testimonies)
    I. Title II. McLeary, Michael P. III. Goldman, Jeanette IV. Series
    940.5318092

ISBN 0-85303-514-8 (paper)

ISSN 1363-3759

Library of Congress Cataloging-in-Publication Data

Akavia, Miriam
    [Ne urim ba-shalekhet. English]
    An End to Childhood/Miriam Akavia: translated from the Hebrew by
    Michael P. McLeary and Jeanette Goldman.
        p. cm. – (The Library of Holocaust testimonies)
    ISBN 0-85303-514-8
    1. Holocaust, Jewish (1939–1945) – Fiction. I. McLeary, Michael P. II.
    Goldman, Jeanette. III. Title. IV. Series.
    PJ5054.A4957N4813 1994
    892.4'36–dc20
                                                                94–18871
                                                                CIP

Typeset in 11/13pt Palatino by FiSH Books, London WC1.
Printed in Great Britain by Halstan & Co, Ltd, Amersham,
Buckinghamshire.

For my sister, Lusia, a twofold gratitude:
first, for her aid in freeing me from the grip
of death in 1945;
and secondly, for her help in freeing
these experiences from within me, many years later.

Contents

Illustrations

The Library of Holocaust Testimonies

It is greatly to the credit of Frank Cass that this series of survivors' testimonies is being published in Britain. The need for such a series has long been apparent here, where many survivors made their homes.

Since the end of the war in 1945 the terrible events of the Nazi destruction of European Jewry have cast a pall over our time. Six million Jews were murdered within a short period; the few survivors have had to carry in their memories whatever remains of the knowledge of Jewish life in more than a dozen countries, in several thousand towns, in tens of thousands of villages and in innumerable families. The precious gift of recollection has been the sole memorial for millions of people whose lives were suddenly and brutally cut off.

For many years, individual survivors have published their testimonies. But many more have been reluctant to do so, often because they could not believe that they would find a publisher for their efforts.

In my own work over the past two decades, I have been approached by many survivors who had set down their memories in writing, but who did not know how to have them published. I realized what a considerable emotional strain the writing down of such hellish memories had been. I also realized, as I read many dozens of such accounts, how important each account was, in its own way, in recounting aspects of the story that had not been told before, and adding to our understanding of the wide range of human suffering, struggle and aspiration.

With so many people and so many places involved, including many hundreds of camps, it was inevitable that the historians and students of the Holocaust should find it difficult at times to grasp the scale and range of these events. The publication of memoirs is therefore an indispensable part of the extension of knowledge, and of public awareness of the crimes that had been committed against a whole people.

Sir Martin Gilbert
Merton College, Oxford

Foreword

Dear Miriam,

This week I returned from your town, from the world where your childhood perished. I returned from a visit to Cracow, where I found your family and friends. Even though most of them were killed, I saw them nevertheless. I saw them in their homes, in the streets and the shops, talking about war and peace, about faith and making a living. I watched them from a distance, hoping against hope that they would be rescued before the enemy reached them with his sword of fire. I thought: perhaps. Perhaps a miracle will happen and a few of them will survive like 'adolescents in autumn', perhaps they will enter your 'vineyard' and find shelter. Perhaps they will succeed in reaching the Promised Land without passing through the halls of Hell.

I had the strangest feeling: around me was Cracow, and I was wandering through your books. You were a faithful companion, Miriam. Thanks to you, I saw letters transformed into living characters.

I have been told that some of your books are going to be translated into Polish. This is good news. It is important for people to remember the Poland of the past. To know that there were once Jews in their country. Beautiful, clever Jewish children; sad, smiling Jewish women. To know that there was once a different childhood in Poland. That there was once a Sabbath in Poland.

I hope that your books will be translated into many different languages. They have a magic of their own, a content of their own. Very few people can write about Jewish children in the war as you do. You reveal and conceal at once their pain, the death they bear within them.

Although you do not actually enter the death camps, somehow the reader feels a strange obligation to enter them with you, or even before you. The kind reader does not want to let you go inside alone. Will he see what you saw? Is anyone capable of understanding what you felt, as a little girl pursued by all the fiends of hell?

Do you remember, Miriam? After the war there were people who tried to make you talk, you and other survivors, in Europe and in Eretz Israel. In vain. Everyone answered in the same utterly weary tone: 'Anyway, you won't understand.'

The same is true today. They won't understand. Only someone who was in Cracow, and fled to Lvov in order to return to Cracow and finally arrived, via Plaszow and Auschwitz, at Bergen-Belsen – only someone who experienced it for himself will understand. Others will not understand. Even if they read all the documentary literature, and see all the films, and speak to all the survivors: they will still be outside looking in. Nevertheless, Miriam, nevertheless, you must go on telling and bearing witness and remembering and reminding – in other words, writing as you have written up to now, in a small, still voice which contains within it the screams of thousands, the mute cry of the silenced.

Maybe then everyone who goes to Cracow will feel as if he is wandering through your books. And everyone who reads your sad, beautiful books will discover in them the Cracow that once existed. And everyone who hears a knock on the door will remember the nights when only a single breath separated the murderer from the redeemer.

Your literary testimony is of the greatest value. It will survive.

Elie Wiesel

Preface

This is the story of a young man, 17 years old, of his experiences during a single month, one month of autumn. The story may well be less than complete, for my inexperienced hand has recorded now what was told me many years ago.

Once, when we were young, he asked me if I believed in reincarnation, in a life after death. I did not really have a clear opinion at the time, and before I could answer he said: 'I believe in it. I have a very strong belief that even when I die, that won't be the absolute end of my existence. In some form or another, something of me will remain.'

Many years have passed since then. Today, when I am reminded of that conversation, and his courageous image appears in my mind, full of the iron will of youth, it seems to me that he was right. I want to believe today that at the moment he was caught up in the cruel torrent of destruction which swept over our people during the Second World War, at that instant his soul was released from its tortured frame. It abandoned his body, rose up over the walls and barbed-wire fences, above the hideous darkness which had enveloped the world, and found freedom. Those of us who knew him can sense his presence within ourselves, and see his image reflected in the figures of our children. His spirit enfolds us, even to this day.

Perhaps these opening lines sound a bit strange to you, as bizarre and extraordinary as the events of those days. But if the beginning is strange, the story is simple: the story of a 17-year-old youth.

To those who were fortunate enough not to have personally experienced the horrors of that period in the flesh, I will add a short note: the story's main character was not called 'Yurek' before the war. His true name was Yeshiyahu, and at home he was called 'Izio', but because he was hiding under false papers, he was forced to use the name appearing on his identity card: Yurek.

Miriam Akavia
Tel Aviv
June 1975

YUREK

Chapter One

Time after time I drag my feet through the noisy streets of the city. The chestnut trees along the avenue are rustling their yellowing leaves, and now and then the cool autumn breeze strengthens, shaking the branches and sending the golden leaves spinning in the air like dancers, to finally let them rest on the ground. Chestnut trees...how I always loved them in bloom, and as they ripened towards autumn. How long ago it was that the chestnuts had fallen, their prickly shells splitting open, when I used to skip so delightedly, gathering the brown, shining fruit as it rolled in the parks of the city where I was born, so far from here...

Now I am no longer gladdened by the sight of these once beloved trees. I don't even notice the beauty of this city through which I wander, all alone. The trees are the same, but I am not the same person any more. In the inner pocket of my coat I carry the new identity card, which states that I am Yurek Kowalik, son of Valery and Bronislawa Kowalik, from Warsaw. This document cost my father a fortune; he bought it with the last of his money, after all his property was stolen, and with it he believed he was buying me the right to live. I feel a sharp pang in my heart whenever I think about my father, who only three years ago was so poised and wise, proud and brave. Today, he is another man altogether. He is still fighting, and has not yet succumbed to fate, but his struggle now seems more like the vain flutterings of a caged bird.

Not knowing exactly where I was, I entered a small, quiet park and sat on a bench. The time seems just to crawl by, and the thought of the long hours of the evening ahead of me makes me shudder. The chill in the air gripped me as I sat, and I wrapped myself tighter within my coat. I made believe that my head was resting on the slight, soft shoulder of Lusinka, my dark young sweetheart, the first and only girlfriend I ever had. I imagined that her face drew near me, that our hands clasped and held...

I had met Lusia only a few months ago, after we were already living in the Ghetto. A group of us, all youngsters expelled from the schools, used to meet and then search, amidst the terrible crowding of the Ghetto, for some corner to use as a 'club', often a cellar or attic. Surprise mingled with pleasure flooded me when I felt the gaze of Lusinka's dark, smiling eyes on my face. At first I thought it was merely a coincidence, that she looked at everyone that way, and I never dreamed that she had a special feeling for me. But it turned out that it was not just chance, and when I realized this, I began to return her glances with my own, very open and admiring. As we started to exchange smiles, we always managed somehow to sit or stand next to one another, depending on the conditions of each particular 'clubhouse'.

Later, we looked for places where we could be alone. Once we found an overturned crate, full of scraps and junk, in a dark little courtyard. We sat there, embracing, with our hands entwined, and I asked: 'Tell me, what is it you see in me? There are so many other boys after you, what made you choose just me?'

Squeezing my hand even tighter, my lovely dark Lusia said: 'Silly goose, do you really want to know? I'm simply crazy about the freckles on your nose...and I love boys who wear glasses, they look so intelligent, and...well, I guess you're just attractive to me, that's all. I...'

Lusia paused here, and I did not press her to finish. I did not want to ruin that beautiful moment. We sat quietly for a bit, then I said: 'You know, when this damned war is over, I'm not going to stay here even one more day. If my parents don't want to leave, or refuse to let me go, I just won't listen to them. I'll get out of this place even if I have to walk for years and live on only grass and water. I'm going to travel until I reach somewhere that you can live differently, a place where, if I ever have a son and name him Moshe, I'll be free to call him "Moishele", as loud as I want.'

'I like the name "Shaike" very much, too,' said my darling girl in a small voice, and she held me even closer. My head was reeling, and through my body rushed waves of delicious warmth, as if I had drunk a glass of fine, old wine.

Could this be love? It was so good sitting with her like this that I did not want to move, for fear that a clumsy movement would spoil some of the pleasure. So I just caressed her shoulders, inhaling deeply the fragrance of her soft, black hair.

Sitting here on the bench in the strange city of Lvov, without a soul in the world close to me, I squeezed my arms around my own body with a strange, grey feeling, half-dreaming and half-awake. I imagined that my beloved girl was in my arms, that I was holding her tightly to me, so she would not leave me here alone, so she would not abandon me...

A hand touches my shoulder, a very real hand. As I open my eyes my body freezes in fear, and my throat becomes constricted, unable to make a sound. Above me stands an elderly man, with a broad face adorned by a well-tended moustache; he is trying to calm me.

'Why so startled, young man? What's there to be afraid of? It looks to me as if you've been working too hard on your mathematics or grammar...go on home now, your parents must be worried about you. A big lad like you doesn't have to sleep on a public park bench. The state of things is getting worse, it's true, but there's no need for that, no need at all. Do you live in this neighbourhood?'

'Yes, uh...no, not exactly in the neighbourhood, but I'll find...I'll just be going...Thank you very much,' I stammered.

'Strange boy,' murmured the man, shrugging his shoulders indifferently. '"Thank you very much", he says; well, what's to thank?'

Even as he was talking to himself, I had begun walking

away. I wanted to run, to vanish from his sight, but I was afraid that would draw his attention or arouse suspicion. I walked with slow, swaying steps, as if I were still drowsy. I was terrified that the man was just playing with me, putting on a front, and that he was in fact investigating me. *Perhaps he already knows all about me, and is on his way to alert the Gestapo. Faster! If only I could just disappear, so he won't know where I'm going! Oh, just leave me alone!*

For half an hour I dodged through streets and alleys in order to lose any pursuer. Only when I was certain that no-one was following me, I headed towards the neighbourhood of the apartment.

The apartment was on Bema Street, on the ground floor of a three-storey building. From the street, a long dark passageway led to the entrance door. The entire apartment consisted of merely a kitchen and one other room; the bathroom was outside, on the other side of the hall. In the kitchen, opposite the entrance door, were the sink and tap; above them hung a shelf with a small, cheap mirror. The kitchen also contained a table and two stools, a large coal stove for cooking, and a bed with several large pillows and a quilt. Beside the bed was the door to the inner room. Across from the door there was a window – to what or where I never knew, for it was always closed and covered by a dark curtain.

The elderly couple who lived in the kitchen served as *Hausmeisters*, and as such were responsible for the cleaning and upkeep of the whole building. During the day, they sat on the stools; at night they slept on the solitary bed in the kitchen. From the stove usually rose steam from the boiling water for tea, or sometimes from boiled potatoes and cabbage – the staple foods of the Polish peasant. The old couple spoke in the melodious Lvov dialect, slightly different from the Polish heard in Cracow, my city. In fact, they rarely spoke at all; they never asked me any questions, and I was grateful for that. Father had provided me with their address when he sent me away. From his contacts he knew of this couple who, for a large sum of money, were willing to give me a bed in their apartment.

I was not the only occupant of the inner room; there were two other beds besides mine, making three altogether. The tenants were not regular: 'Everyone is looking for something more...pleasant.' Most said that they were coming to stay only for one or two nights. For the four days since I had arrived, however, the tenants had not changed.

I didn't know much about the two other men who, like myself, slipped silently beneath their blankets every night, asking no questions, revealing nothing. In spite of this, I was able to learn a little about them, particularly in the mornings, as I observed their faces and clothing.

One of them – whom I called in my mind 'the Scratcher' – was two, maybe three, years older than me, very tall and thin, his face pale and covered with swollen pimples. I didn't know where he was from, or what he did each day. We saw one another only in the morning, before leaving the apartment, each on his own way. I tried to think of him as 'Aryan',* for I wanted him also to consider me as such. He once told me that he was *Volksdeutsch*,** and he possessed a German identity card to prove it.

The second tenant was a man about 32 years old, very strong and in the prime of his life, with a ruddy complexion and reddish-blond hair. Each morning he would pull on a pair of shining, black leather boots, along with the uniform of the SS, with the swastika on his coat. I didn't speak very much with him either, but I knew more about him. I knew, of course, that he wasn't an SS soldier at all, that he was a Jew like me. But even in my mind I never dared to call him Jewish, as if merely the thought was liable to lead to disaster. He was my father's contact, and through him we had obtained my new identity card. This man, older than both of us, was a figure of authority for us, owing to his age and outwardly confident bearing.

From time to time he gave us much-needed advice. He especially stressed one thing: 'Don't get close to each other. We

*Aryan: in the context of this book, non-Jewish.
** *Volksdeutsch*: of German extraction.

have no choice but to survive each on his own. Otherwise, if one of us gets into trouble, we are all lost. The less we are connected with one another, the better our chances of staying alive. The old folks won't turn us in, first because they're making a fortune out of us, and second, because they know very well that if it is proved that they sheltered us, they'll be dealt with mercilessly. They took the chance, and now they're in the same boat with us.'

He was called Miller, Hans Miller, and in my head I labelled him 'the SS man'. The other's name was Maximilian. At the outset I had thought that if two nationalities were already represented in this strange room, maybe I should declare myself a Ukrainian. The Ukrainians enjoyed a privileged status during the Nazi occupation. In Lvov, according to what I had heard, the Ukrainians functioned as 'bloodhounds' for the Germans in the search for hidden Jews. It was said here in Lvov that 'A German can't tell the difference between a Jew and non-Jew, but a Ukrainian call smell a Jew instantly, and hands him over without a qualm.' Other than this, however, I knew nothing about the Ukrainians, and therefore decided to remain Yurek, a Pole, whose parents had fallen in the battle for the defence of Warsaw, now arrived in Lvov by way of Cracow in search of his aunt, his mother's sister, whom he had not yet succeeded in finding. I repeated this story to myself over and over again, many times, like an actor repeating his lines before a play.

As I entered the room this time I found it darkened, stuffy. My two roommates were sitting together on one bed and, uncharacteristically, whispering. When they saw me they fell silent, not including me in their secrets. Apparently I was still not to be completely trusted in their eyes. Hans took a crumpled note from his pocket and gave it to me without a word; a few lines, unsigned, in a slanted handwriting. I knew the author immediately – Father! My heart skipped a beat as I eagerly read:

Go to Stanowski's Pharmacy on Pilsotsky St. and request the prescription for Ledwon. We are well.

The men began to whisper again. I took off my outer clothing, arranged it at the foot of my bed, and fell asleep. The precious note I held clasped tightly in my hand.

When I awoke the following morning, the room was deserted. In the kitchen, the old couple were moving about as usual. I was pleased to save myself the daily wait in line for washing my face and hands at the kitchen sink. The old folks paid no attention to me. I wondered when I would be able to wash the rest of my body.

I went out into the street without having eaten a thing. The city was already awake, despite the early hour. Trolley buses passed, jammed with passengers. Those my age and younger off to school, the adults off to work. Outside the shops trailed long queues of housewives waiting for their rations of food. My stomach growled, and I could have easily eaten a whole loaf of bread if I'd had one. I was still without a ration book, because I was not yet registered on the list of residents. I kept putting off the registration until I could find a job, being afraid of places where they demanded an identity card and asked questions. Just then I had only one objective: to find Pilsotsky Street and to meet the pharmacist. After nearly an hour's walk I arrived, only to find the pharmacy still closed. I thought it unwise to wait there for the pharmacist; it would be better to make a circuit around the area and return after a while, to enter as a normal customer. I decided to use this time to find something solid to eat.

A few blocks away was a small market, which offered fresh milk, potatoes and cabbage, and also home-baked bread in round loaves. I bought a quarter loaf of bread and a piece of white cheese, resolving always to carry a cup in future, so that I could also buy milk and drink it on the spot. At home we always boiled the milk to guard against bacteria, but to hell with nonsense like that – to be afraid of bacteria in these times struck me as truly ridiculous.

After two hours had passed I returned to Pilsotsky Street. The pharmacy was now open, and the entrance bell tinkled as I walked in. On the other side of the counter stood the pharmacist in his white coat, wrapping a small package for the woman who had entered before me. She paid him, and stepped up on the scale as she made her exit, sighing: 'Losing weight, still losing weight...'

The pharmacist smiled and said nothing. All this time I stood and gazed at the toothbrushes beneath the glass, as if choosing one for myself. When the lady had left, I approached the pharmacist and asked, in the calmest voice I could muster, for the prescription for Mr Ledwon.

The man eyed me for a long moment, and I bore his gaze in quiet expectation.

'We must talk,' he said. 'If someone comes in, I'll prescribe you some pills for diarrhoea. Try not to get confused.'

I nodded my head in understanding.

'You're from Cracow?' he questioned.

'Right.'

'Ledwon told me about you. I assume he also informed you about us, that you know what we're doing.'

My brain was racing. No-one had told me about the pharmacist Stanowski from Lvov, or about his activities, but I knew very well what Ledwon was doing secretly in Cracow.

'Yes,' I replied, 'I know what you're doing.'

'Good. We need students like you. We have a lot of work to do, especially decoding, duplicating, distributing, and...also special missions. But about these in due time. Do your parents know that you've volunteered for the underground?'

From this question I concluded that Mr Stanowski did not know I was Jewish. At that moment, to my good fortune, someone entered, and the pharmacist continued quite naturally: '...take these three times a day and drink a lot of hot tea.'

'Thank you,' I returned. *A cup of hot tea wouldn't hurt right now*, I thought.

'I'd also like to buy a toothbrush.'

'By all means. Here, choose one yourself,' he said, placing a packet before me.

After the customer had left, the pharmacist went on: 'We're working in several branches, each made up of several families. I'll attach you to the Gronowski family; they'll be responsible for filling you in on things, starting you off in the work. I'll receive mail for you here. It will be passed to me through Ledwon. You can also send letters to Cracow through me, because the regular mail is all checked by a censor; the bastards have us by the throat, but they won't break our spirit.'

I was excited at the prospect of the work which awaited me, and ready to begin at once; I hoped they would give me as much as possible to do. Fed up with the prolonged lack of activity, I resolved not to avoid any mission, no matter how dangerous.

'Is there any hopeful news?' I asked Stanowski.

'Unfortunately, no; the news is very bad. You'll hear it all at the Gronowskis'.'

He passed me a letter for Wanda and Kazimesh Gronowski; their address he gave me verbally. He also handed me a letter from home – without the sender's address, of course. Again my heart was in my throat at the sight of my father's slanted handwriting. Stanowski and I agreed that I would come twice a week to the pharmacy to send and receive mail. I left with the two letters in the inner pocket of my coat, next to my breast. First of all, I wanted to find a safe spot in which to be alone with the letter from home.

Dear son,

It hasn't been a week since we parted, yet it seems already an eternity. I know it's even harder on you, but believe me, there's no other way, simply no other choice. Here there is next to no chance at all, though we can't just sit with our hands folded, without trying to do something. I'm working to fulfil the plan we discussed before you left. Ania will arrive on Thursday, 5 November, 1942, on the express train which reaches Lvov at 5:00 in the afternoon. Wait for her at the station, and take care of her. Take care of yourself, too, and I pray that God will watch over you both.

We are all well, except that everything looks so hopeless here. I pray I'm wrong about that. Ania will tell you all about our situation. I'm sending some things with her, and money as well. You'll have to live on a tight budget, for there's no telling when I'll be able to send more, if at all. I want to believe that the people I've made contacts with won't desert you, now that I can no longer help you. I feel such remorse at the thought of the opportunities I had and failed to exploit; I'm tormented by the decisions I put off again and again until it was too late. I hope you'll believe that I always wanted what was best for you, even though I could never have imagined that it would come to this.

I'll try to write again, by way of Ledwon-Stanowski, or directly through the Lvov post. Send your letters through Stanowski. Don't forget to meet Ania. Take care of yourselves, my children.

There was no signature at the end, likewise no address.

I sat on a bench, desolate, facing the red wall of the Lvov post office. As I finished the letter, I had difficulty swallowing the lump in my throat, caused by the tears which would not quite flow. The whole state of affairs was so depressing, but hardest of all to bear was what my father was going through, how his role had been undermined, his spirit broken. At that moment, I myself badly needed encouragement and support, yet I had nowhere to turn for them, now that Father saw me as the last hope, the only and final chance to realize his complicated and risky plan to save our family. I would have preferred to be there with the others, anything rather than being so isolated, so lonely. But Father said that there was no hope left where they were, no chance, no turning back. He asked me to forgive him; I could not understand that – what should I forgive him for? Was he to blame for what was happening? True, in the past I had been angry more than once with Father. He really used to get on my back sometimes: 'Sit up straight! You don't hold a pen like that! You'd better start learning to use your right hand. Don't talk with your mouth full! Work on your grades in mathematics!' and on he went. Father demanded a lot from me, more than he asked from the girls.

If only I could suffer all that again, if only he would scold me now. How good it would be to hear his 'Sit up straight! Eat properly!' and I'd obey just to please him, to pull him out of his awful depression. Or maybe he was asking my forgiveness for not sending me to the agricultural school? I think it was called 'Mikveh Israel'. Mother wrote there once and received a favourable reply, but Father wanted me to be an engineer, not a farmer. My mother also wanted all of us, long before the war, to emigrate to Eretz Israel, suggesting to Father that we buy an orchard and all work on it together. Father used to smile tolerantly at her and say: 'We'll go, but not to break our backs in a fruit orchard. That's not for us old folks. I'm planning it all. The children are learning Hebrew. When they grow up, they'll go first, and we'll follow after them.'

Perhaps it's for this he wants forgiveness, for the wrong plan, for the bitter mistake he made. Oh Father, Father, how wonderful it would be if we were now in some sun-washed settlement in the Promised Land! I wouldn't be all alone then, here in this damned city of Lvov, and you wouldn't all be in that even more miserable place. I'm so glad my sister, Ania, is coming in another two days. It's a shame that such a delicate girl must come to this rough life; it won't really suit her very well. But I'm happy that finally there will be someone close to me, somebody with whom I can talk. Where will I take her? But then again, do I have any choice? When Ania arrives I'll look for another place for us. I just wish she was here already!

I tried to cheer myself up, deciding to visit the Gronowskis in the two days remaining before her arrival – a visit in which I had already placed a lot of hope. I felt renewed, once again full of courage and optimism. Sitting down at one of the tables running along the walls of the main lobby of the post office, I wrote a few lines to those at home:

> Dear everyone,
>   I received your letter dated 2.11.42. I'm very happy that Ania is coming here. Don't worry, we'll manage. I feel great, and lack nothing. I hope to find suitable work soon in order to support us. I'll also try to work out our plans to the end, particularly as regards the children. I just need a little time to get settled in a job and find a better apartment. I miss you all terribly; the homesickness is what afflicts me the most. But I'm hanging on. Take care of yourselves. I love you.

Folding the letter, I put it in my pocket and headed in the direction of Stanowski's Pharmacy, to give it to him. I had a blank envelope, and I addressed it when I reached the pharmacy.

Thinking that it would be best to arrive at the Gronowskis' around four in the afternoon, I did not hurry especially. It was raining outside, with a chilly wind that penetrated up my sleeves and around my collar. I turned the collar up, and lengthened my stride.

The Gronowski family lived in a modern building situated in a completely new quarter of the city. A broad, clean stairwell enclosed the steps up to their third-floor apartment. As I went up, I tried to guess what they would look like, but I had nothing on which to build an impression; I knew absolutely nothing about them. It was hard to try to compare them with any of my own acquaintances, for I knew few adults. My imagination simply failed me at this point. Each time I tried to see them as one of my relatives I immediately rejected the comparison.

Our family, one of the largest and oldest Jewish families in Cracow, contained a wide variety of characters. In fact, almost the entire spectrum of beliefs and lifestyles were represented within it. Among my mother's three brothers, one was extremely religious, both in outlook and in practice, the second voiced sentiments with a leftist flavour, and the third was a traditional, observant Jew, but lived a modern life, enjoying music, poetry, and dancing. Of my father's four sisters, one was married to a genuine Hasid and, of course, wore a wig. She refused to eat in any home but her own, even if she knew the kitchen to be kosher. The second sister, while still young, left her family and city to emigrate to Eretz Israel, and the two youngest sisters vacillated even now between Zionism and assimilation.

The widow of Father's brother lived with her two children in the city of Hshanow, not far from Cracow. Her son grew up as a *yeshiva* student. My mother's cousins were completely assimilated; some of them emigrated from Poland, while a few lived in Cracow and worked in the free trades. They retained no contact at all with Judaism. Among my father's cousins were some who continued in their parents' tradition, the petit-bourgeois life of Cracow, others who studied in universities, and still others who were either religious or assimilated. A few were wealthy, a handful leftists, and there were even some who wandered about barefoot and milked cows on a Zionist preparatory farm; a few of the latter actually emigrated to Eretz Israel.

But I still could not fit the image of the Gronowskis with any of these types. I had known some non-Jews as well; my teachers in the local primary school were Polish (my high school studies I completed in the Hebrew grammar school), but I knew them only within the narrow framework of teacher and pupil, never finding the opportunity to speak with them on a more personal level. I naturally came to know the Polish housekeepers who worked in our home before the war. With them, I was actually on very friendly terms, but I could not bring myself to believe that Mrs Gronowski resembled any of them, or that Mr Gronowski would look like Pavel or Antony, or any of the others who had worked for Father before the war.

My thoughts finally settled on the Kalitsky family, our former neighbours. They were middle-aged, a cultured and exclusive couple, and with them I never exchanged more than a 'Good evening' or 'Good morning' on the stairs. I assumed that Mr and Mrs Gronowski would be at least the age of my parents, if not older.

Hence I was very surprised when a young woman, 22 at most, with blonde hair cut in a short, girlish hairstyle, answered the doorbell. I stood in their doorway, flustered, and was saved from my confusion by a vigorous young male voice from within.

'What is it, Wandziu? Why are you keeping our visitor waiting on the stairway? Tell him to please come in.'

Presently I met the source of the voice himself, his hand outstretched in greeting with a smile. Feeling relieved already, I removed from my pocket the letter Stanowski had given me. Gronowski's quick glance instantly recognized the handwriting, and he became even more friendly.

'Come in, please! Here's a place to hang your coat. Please, make yourself comfortable.'

As I was hanging my coat, the couple read the short note. Gronowski again shook my hand.

'My name's Kazimesh, but everyone calls me "Kazik"; why don't you, too?'

'Yurek.' I introduced myself.

'Great, Yurek. Let's sit down and talk a bit. Wanda, dear, won't you make us a cup of tea, please?'

We sat in the warm, pleasant room, in comfortable armchairs, drinking the sweet, fragrant tea and talking. Kazik did not offer me any alcohol, whether out of consideration for my age or because of the short supplies at that time, I don't know. Yet even without a drink I was intoxicated, drunk in the warm, homely atmosphere and presence of these two young, intelligent people. Meeting them was a healing balm for all the days I had spent in frosty, cold isolation. Plus another thing I was unprepared for – they treated me as a grown up, an equal, despite the fact that I was at least five years younger than Wanda, and seven younger than Kazik.

They described to me their underground activities, the network of which they were a part. At six p.m., we gathered silently around the radio receiver, listening to the 'Voice of Poland', broadcasting in exile from London. There were many disturbances during the broadcast, much static and shrill interference. With great difficulty I managed to catch details of the movements of the armies, political statements from America and other places, and words of encouragement for occupied Poland and its people. But not a single word was said about the plight of the Jews in Poland.

Quiet reigned as the broadcast ended. In my own silence were mingled feelings of relief and disappointment, for nothing had been said about what was for me the most important of all issues. The meaning of the couple's silence was unclear to me; at any rate, I was glad they did not begin immediately to discuss and analyse the situation. For nearly two years now I had been cut off from the free world, and of what was happening outside the Cracow Ghetto I knew very little. I failed to understand how so many armies could lose to a single one; where were all the heroes, the great commanders? Where were all the international organizations, how could they allow this to happen? Why had Russia become Germany's ally in 1939? Couldn't they see through the shrewd propaganda of Hitler?

If Wanda and Kazik had begun talking over the state of affairs, I would have been hard-pressed just then to hide my disorientation. One terrible and bitter fact was quite clear, however: they were annihilating us, and not in battle or at the front, but no-one was lifting a finger in our defence. Following the armies' movements, empathizing with the suffering of the conquered peoples, was all very well for Kazik and Wanda in their lovely apartment, with their full stomachs. But for me there was no respite. *I'm a fugitive, hunted, with the danger of death lurking constantly around me. I can't suffer the pain of the rest of the world – my own suffering is a burden almost too heavy to bear.*

I was grateful to my hosts for not inquiring too much about me. They warmly invited me to come again the following day, saying that they wanted to include me in their activities, and I told them I was willing to do any sort of work they wanted. I was reluctant to leave their warm, safe nest for the cold street, so foreign and menacing. Less than anything else did I want to return to the unfriendly room, with its two strangers and the mutual suspicion between us, added to the threat of death which hung, suspended, in the air. But looking at my watch, I saw that it was time to go.

'Is there anything you need?' asked Kazik suddenly, before we parted.

'No,' I answered. 'I don't need anything – for the time being,' I added, with a weak smile.

'Don't worry, my boy,' said Kazik in his genial fashion, 'and don't forget our address. Tomorrow, Wanda will make us a dinner, isn't that right, dear?'

'Oh, you men...' chuckled Wanda. 'It's no joke that the way to a man's heart is through his stomach! Is there something in particular you'd like for dinner, Yurek? Just say so, and I'll try to make it.'

'Yes, of course.' I even surprised myself with my bright reply. 'I'd very much like roast duck with all the trimmings, and as an appetizer, uh..., caviare would be nice.'

The three of us burst out laughing. Wanda winked at me.

'I'm making a list, my dear. One hour after the war's over, your request will be granted in full.'

As I watched them, standing there in the entrance to the apartment with their arms linked and grins on their faces, I remembered Ania's imminent arrival.

'A friend of mine is coming from Cracow in another two days,' I said, and then immediately regretted the words. But they did not press me for more information, leaving the admission as it stood.

'You'll have to tell us about her some time, if you like.'

Ania, Annushia...here she is, stepping off the train, a little pale, with dark shadows under her eyes. She's wearing a dark blue coat, like that of a schoolgirl, and her blonde hair flows out from under her beret, also dark blue. I run towards her, forcing my way through the crowds of people streaming in all directions in the railway station. From the moment I caught sight of Ania my heart began pounding, flooding my veins with warm, pleasurable waves; a tremor ran through my whole body, a tingling which spoke of home, family.

Ania's eyes found mine. Even from a distance, I could see her relief. A man in a grey overcoat was helping her remove her luggage. I approach and hug Ania, rather awkwardly; she is also unsure how to act, what is permitted, what may be forbidden. Our meeting, which should have been so filled with emotion, seems lukewarm, even cool. Only in her eyes is she speaking, and she feels how my heart goes out to her. Her eyes say: 'Wait until later, I've so much to tell you, about everyone, everything...'

'Thank you very much, sir,' Ania said to her companion, as he laid her suitcase beside her. 'Here, you see, someone is expecting me. We'll manage with the basket.'

'Nothing doing,' replied the man. 'How will the two of you be able to handle that large basket? At least let me help take it off the train. We had better hurry, the train's about to move.'

I jump up after him into the coach which Ania had emerged from. I see a huge wicker basket, closed with a latch and lock, a very familiar basket indeed. In more pleasant times, we used to pack our things in it when we travelled for the long summer holidays to Zakopaneh, or to Rabka or Mushina on the Poprad River. Two porters would come then to take the basket down from the apartment to the carriage in which we were travelling. It was so large that it would not fit into a regular coach.

Why had Ania brought this gigantic basket...? But there was no time for questions now. With a considerable effort, we succeed in lowering the basket onto the platform. The man, breathing heavily, asks: 'What now?'

'We'll get a porter,' the two of us answer quickly. 'It's fine, we'll manage. Thank you so much, sir, really, thank you!'

The man shrugs his shoulders, admitting that he has to hurry to meet his wife and children, and goes on his way after wishing us good luck.

From the other direction, two SS soldiers are drawing near to us. They step sharply along in their black, shiny boots, marching in step; left, right, left. The people on the platform recoiled instinctively before them, and a space automatically formed along both sides of their path. We froze on the spot; the basket undoubtedly attracted attention, and because of it we could not mingle with the crowd. To make things worse, there was no porter in sight.

'What's in this basket?' I muttered under my breath, suddenly angry.

'Bedspreads and pillowcases, embroidered tablecloths, needlework...' Ania's voice was quavering, on the verge of tears.

We were lucky; the SS men did not notice us, and moved away from the area.

'Embroidered tablecloths and needlework,' I sighed. 'Just what we need here...Listen, we have to get away from here as quickly as possible, without attracting any more attention. So what are we going to do?'

Ania placed her suitcase on top of the basket, grabbed one of its handles, and said: 'Come on, let's carry it.'

We succeeded in dragging it a few metres but it became clear that this was not the solution. I was afraid to leave Ania alone with the basket; otherwise, I would have gone off to find a station handcart.

As I was still trying to decide what to do, Ania went up to a man in a railway uniform and asked in a childish manner: 'Sir, could we possibly get help in taking that basket out of the station?'

Her approach evidently pleased the railway worker. He looked at Ania, then at the basket, and finally at me.

'What's this, are you two moving a bunch of Jewish treasure?'

Again, my heart stood still, but Ania answered without hesitation: 'Oh no, actually, it belongs to my grandmother; she has just sold her house in the country.'

'Wait here a moment,' said the worker. 'I'll arrange some sort of transport for you.'

In a few minutes he returned with a baggage cart and helped us move the basket to the left luggage office. I offered to pay him, and he did not refuse. I also paid the storage fee for the basket and got a receipt.

Only now do we breathe a little easier.

'Come on,' I tell Ania. 'Let's get out of here fast.'

In one hand I took up Ania's suitcase, while with the other I held her hand and led her out of the station. After all the gates and checkpoints were behind us, we felt much more secure.

But now a new dilemma confronted us: where to go? Ania was bound to be tired out, but I did not want to bring her directly to the apartment in Bema Street. I wanted to talk with her first, and besides, she must be hungry; for that matter, I would not object to some sort of meal myself.

'Let's go,' I said, like a true knight. 'I'm taking you out to dinner.' We walked a moment in silence.

'Have you by any chance seen Lusia Bossak in the last few days?' My voice was strangely hoarse. Ania shook her head.

'No,' she replied sadly. 'Not so long ago, we used to meet sometimes at Optima Court to play volleyball. Now, even that's impossible. It's so terribly crowded; people bump into one another and hardly notice each other's faces.'

What a let-down, I thought with a pang. *I wonder if I'll hear about her soon? Will I ever see her again?* To Ania I said:

'Can you tell me about Mother, Father, Reli, Grandmother, and the children?'

'Father's so discouraged, you know, it's just terrible to see him like that. He wanted to shut himself and all of us into the kitchen and turn on the gas. He meant to do it, quite seriously.

He said it would be better than what was waiting for us. But Mother rebelled; imagine, our mother, who had always submitted to his every wish, this time shouted and said it was wrong, forbidden, that there was still hope. Tell me, Yur, do you think our plan to save the family will work? Because back there, the situation is so horrible...'

'I don't know, but I want you to tell me every last detail, everything that has happened since I left the house. But maybe not just now. Let's go and eat and then get some sleep. Tomorrow, we'll worry about the basket, and we'll talk. We have to settle on a plan of action.'

'Father did give me all sorts of instructions about how to deal with our money. But I'm really tired to death.'

'Come on, then, in another hour you'll be in bed.'

We ate a light and tasteless meal in a rundown restaurant. Afterwards, I brought Ania to the Bema Street flat. I told the old people that they would receive an extra sum for her. Without a word, they brought another camp bed from the basement (I also slept on a camp bed) and put it in the middle of the room, for the other three beds were ranged along the walls. Ania was exhausted, and I was relieved that she could not pay any attention to the room or its occupants. She lay down, and was instantly asleep.

I slept very badly that night. In addition to my own personal worries, I now felt the burden of responsibility for Ania. The news from home disturbed me more than anything else, and I was eager to hear even the minutest details. All that had befallen us since the start of the war passed before my eyes over and over again...

Chapter Two

The first German bombs fell on 1 September 1939, right in our neighbourhood of Cracow. Hearing the drone of the planes, we all rushed to the windows to look, sure that it was an exercise of the Polish Air Force. I was the first to discern the swastika on the wings of the low-flying planes. When I told Mother she did not believe me, thinking that I was, as usual, daydreaming, but only a moment later my father called from his office and informed us that war had broken out and that German infantry had already crossed the Polish border. After a few minutes there was a tremendous explosion and every window in our lovely apartment was shattered. The Germans bombed at random, and many of the casualties were civilians – the air-raid sirens began only after the bombing had already ceased.

Panic reigned in the city; no-one knew what to do. Father returned from the office, his face ashen; he had driven himself home in the carriage drawn by our beloved white horse. He ordered us to pack only the bare necessities of clothing and food, for 'we're moving to a quieter section of the city'. There, he felt, we'd be more secure. We quickly made up a few bundles and abandoned our beautiful home with its broken windows, climbing into the carriage. Father sat in the coachman's seat, and beside him sat Mother, hugging the shaken Ania, then only eleven and a half years old. Reli, who was 15, and I, 14, were seated in the back of the carriage, to watch the luggage.

On the outskirts of the city, on Hocimska Street, my father had built a small apartment house, which he completed in 1938. He had rented all the rooms but one, on the ground floor; it was to this apartment that he was bringing us now.

To our surprise, when we arrived we found the apartment occupied. Yozef, the janitor and caretaker, who lived in a small hut in the courtyard, had decided on his own to move his family into this more modern flat in the new building. He now regarded us with overt hostility, a complete change from the usual meek, obsequious manner which he and his wife had always displayed towards us in the past. Against his will, he moved out of the apartment, with much grumbling and abuse, muttering something to the effect that 'the Germans will soon teach you Jews a lesson...'.

On the radio we heard the famous poem about Athens under siege, the speech of Melchiades to the frightened people. He spoke of ancient Greece, of the war of the few against the many, and of the heroic choice of an honourable death rather than a life of humiliation:

> He who chooses a life of slavery, that man chooses a dog's life; he puts a rope around his neck and grovels, abject and humiliated, at the feet of those who kick him.
>
> But we, trapped together, are united in our common distress, and we will attack and crush our enemies, or, if it be the will of the gods, we shall find our shelter in the grave, dead but still free. Only the wreaths of victory shall grace our brows, or the pale cast of death – but never the blush of shame.
>
> Our nation's glorious past calls us to battle, every lump of this soil for which our fathers have fought, these skies which witnessed the might of our heroes; to battle our proud heritage exhorts us, to the end. The gods are with us, they will give us strength and defend us from death and disgrace.
>
> Let it, then, be said by all: Victory or Death!

The poem made a strong impression, giving us the feeling that someone was indeed defending us on the borders, that all would turn out well. But the illusion was as brief as a dream; the radio now began to broadcast instructions about the blackout, about the painting of lights, hanging of black curtains, and the covering of the windows. Volunteers were called for, to help dig trenches for defence purposes. Civil defence officials began to run about, checking basements, teaching the use of gas masks and basic principles of first aid.

As dusk fell we heard, at a distance but still quite clearly, the thunder of artillery. Rumours said that the Germans were advancing almost without resistance. The Polish soldiers were left on the front without officers, and as a result, simply turned and ran for their lives. Added to the ranks of soldiers streaming eastward were masses of civilians, on foot or in horse-drawn carriages. The word was that the arrival of the Germans meant only shortages and hardship for all, and for the Jews – death. Everyone said that they would kill all the Jews, by shooting, hanging, or any other possible means, but first they would starve, humiliate and torture them.

On the small lane where we had found our shelter lived very few Jews, but the shock-waves had reached even them; everyone had to escape as soon as possible. Those who delayed in order to try to salvage property and bank accounts, or to try to determine what was happening to their relatives, would not only fail to save either money or family, but were also risking their own lives. The rush was on to pack knapsacks, put on comfortable shoes, leave the city and head eastward, fleeing the Germans.

'I can't go,' declared my mother, her eyes pleading for justification from Father. 'I simply can't.'

Ania and Reli stood at her side, hugging her.

'Nothing terrible will happen to us. It's just not possible that they mean to...with people like us. We won't bother anyone. They'll surely just leave us alone; besides, everyone says that it's the men who are in the greatest danger.'

The knapsacks for Father and me are already packed. Father speaks in a whisper with my mother, goes out in the street to check a few things, and then finally turns to me: 'We're on our way.'

Mother and Father embrace for a long moment. She smooths my hair and kisses me. The girls cling to Father, covering him with goodbye kisses. All our eyes are moist.

We set out on the street leading east from the city, towards the Bogue River. Beyond the Bogue were the Russians, who had attacked Poland from the east by surprise, and halted near the river in accordance with an agreement made with the Germans. We were very soon engulfed in the flood of civilians rushing eastward. From streets and alleys, from nearly every house more people emerge, all with their faces turned to the east, towards a safer place. The current grows ever wider; mingled in the crowd are those on foot as well as carriages piled high with bundles, heavily loaded. People toss their things on the carts of strangers, then walk alongside them. Once in a while, someone even manages to jump onto one of the carriages. Cars drive into the stream, their horns blaring, nearly running down the walkers; they are cursed by those on foot. Family members strive to remain together, and retreating soldiers blend into the crush of women and children.

Father and I hold hands tightly, to avoid losing one another. He is not drifting with the tide; I can feel somehow that he is hesitating. Father does not push ahead with the rest; instead, he is worried at the thought of those left behind, Mother and the girls. To flee – even to save our lives – was simply not possible for him.

On every side we are being shoved, sworn at.

'Get moving! What are you standing there for, anyway?'

Get moving? To where? Nobody really knows at this point.

'That does it,' said Father suddenly. 'I just can't go without them.'

So we turned around and headed back. With great difficulty we pushed our way against the tide of people. In the small hours of the morning, we finally made it back to the apartment on Hocimska Street.

'I just couldn't,' says Father to my mother; this time it was his face that pleaded for justification. Mother falls on his neck, and then on mine. Reli and Ania are laughing through their tears.

Just after dawn, the German Army entered Cracow. I ran with Reli and Ania to the main avenue which intersected the road serving as the western entrance to the city. We stood there on the sidewalk, our eyes wide with amazement; an endless snake of dark green uniforms and steel helmets slithered forward. Its beginning was already lost to view, nor could we see the end of the serpent; it seemed as if there wasn't one. Tired, dusty from the long journey and battles, the strangers still marched in perfect ranks.

We were part of a crowd of civilians, their faces pale, who looked with scornful and threatening expressions on these conquerors, for whom the Polish people have a hatred many generations old. One woman bursts forward into the street, screaming hysterically with her arms held out sideways, insanely hoping somehow to block their way with her own body. A soldier strikes her, she falls, and the snake-like procession moves on, undisturbed: cars, motorcycles, tanks, then more legs…

Enough! ENOUGH! I can't bear to watch it any longer!

That same day, we returned to our apartment on Lotzowska Street. The windows that were broken had been repaired in the meantime. In the parks throughout the city, German soldiers stretched out on the grass, and the air resounded with the alien sound of the German tongue, harsh and full of arrogance.

From that time on, events seemed to pick up speed and momentum. Marinia, our fine housekeeper, who had worked faithfully in our home for five years, just disappeared, vanished without even saying goodbye, as if we were lepers.

A German citizen was sent to our apartment the following

morning: Herr Grada, a minor official in the Occupation administration. He came with an official notice from the Occupation authorities ordering us to give him a room. We put him into Father's study, with its large glass-covered desk, comfortable armchair, a sizeable sofa with an end-table, and a wall cabinet. This cabinet had wooden as well as glass doors, and behind these our books were arranged; our small library included many holy books – the Five Books of Moses, the Gemarrah, and others – along with (ironically) some German classics, a few traditional Polish novels, and two beautifully bound volumes of *The Home Physician*.

The German quickly settled into this cosy room, and from the very first moment filled it with the reek of cigars. Every morning, we had to bring him coffee. Mother would prepare it in our best coffee service, put it on a tray covered with a white napkin, and then send Ania into his room with the tray. After his coffee, Herr Grada would leave for work, to return only in the evening. On his radio set in the study we secretly listened to the news from the BBC.

France had entered the war, and England had also declared war on Germany. Following this news, the broadcasters and war analysts predicted a swift end to the conflict; the Germans boasted of their *Blitzkrieg* or lightning warfare – it would undoubtedly resemble this, but the Germans would be on the losing side.

Meanwhile, more civilian regulations were enacted, mainly against the Jews. Jews must hand over all their money and jewellery; any Jew found with gold, cash or jewels in his possession would be shot.

Worried friends began to come to our apartment to consult with Father. On our street, some four houses from ours, stood a large, new building, its exterior finished with shiny black ceramic tiles. All its tenants were Polish scientists and scholars. During the first days of the occupation of Cracow, they were evicted from their apartments, and along with their families were expelled from the city. The rumour was that they had all been shot – that this was how the Germans tried to 'cleanse' the city of its intelligentsia and reduce to negligible the threats of any rebellion against them.

Father again considers an escape over the border. The word is that by way of Czechoslovakia one could escape to Rumania, and from there make one's way across the sea. This sort of daring exploit was organized by professional escape artists from the underworld, and would certainly cost a family like ours a fortune. Father acts quickly. Not having enough cash on hand, he therefore decides without hesitation to sell our house on Hocimska Street. Offering the house at a ridiculously low price, he finds a buyer. The purchaser and his agent come to our house in the afternoon with the money, and the contract for the transaction is signed. The escape organizer is supposed to come the following day, receive the money, and give us detailed instructions for the journey.

Only a few hours after the deal was completed, however, a furious knocking is heard at our door. I rush to open it, and am dumbstruck to see a short, uniformed German with a hard rubber baton in his belt, and a revolver in his hand. Behind him are several Polish thugs who have already managed to secure for themselves a pin with the *Volksdeutsch* insignia on it; we had been basely betrayed, either by the buyer or by his agent.

'The money! The cash! Where is it?'

The German orders us all to stand with our faces to the wall and hands raised, prodding us with his loaded pistol. The treacherous Poles ravage the apartment, literally turn it upside down, opening cupboards and drawers and throwing everything onto the floor.

Father cannot bear it, just standing with his face to the wall and hands upraised. He turns around, trying to say something, and then the fat, ignorant German immediately slapped him across the face, with all his strength, the filthy animal. My father's face is pale, but without a trace of fear. He stands ready for anything, and acts courageously, despite the clear knowledge that any second he could get a bullet through his skull. Ania suddenly breaks away from the wall and rushes to his side, in tears, trying to defend him. Mother and Reli burst out crying, and I...I wished the earth would open up and swallow me, so that I could not see my father, so proud and brave, standing there stricken and mortified.

At this point, after the bastards had pushed us around and ransacked our home, they decide to negotiate. Hoping that they will not succeed in uncovering all the money he received for the house, Father promises to bring in a few minutes the sum they are demanding. He sends Ania to the bakery of his friend, Landau, the father of Ania's friend, Christine, in order to request from him a loan of a few thousand zlotys. Ania races on her way, only the sense of the importance of her mission keeping her from stumbling. At the bakery, she tells Mr Landau what is happening at our home. He gives her the money without hesitation, and she runs back on her last breaths, fearing that she will be too late.

When she arrives back at the apartment, it is empty of strangers. Father is sitting, his hands gripping his bowed head as if it were liable to tumble off his shoulders. He just sits, motionless, like a statue, his face a study of pain and anguish. Mother, Reli and I move about on tiptoe, trying to clean up the apartment. Ania appears at the door with the bundle of money.

'There's no need, now,' I tell her. 'You had better go back to Mr Landau's in a few minutes. They've found and taken it all.'

That was the end of our escape plan.

A new order was issued: all Jews must wear a white armband with a blue Star of David on their right arm. The next day, Jews were forbidden to ride on the trolley buses. Then it was also prohibited for Jewish children to study in Polish schools.

Reli and I were studying at the Hebrew grammar school, so this last ruling affected only Ania, who was in the sixth grade at a Polish elementary school. Ania was upset.

'I didn't even get to say goodbye to my teacher or to my friends...'

'That's all right,' my mother consoled her. 'You'll soon be back at school, anyway.'

Because Reli and I were long-standing students at the Hebrew school, our parents succeeded in enrolling Ania, too. So the three of us began each day to walk to school from Lobzowska to Bshozowa Street, on the opposite side of town. Ania is very disorientated, not being used to the noise and uproar of the Hebrew school. In the playground, before the first lessons, boys and girls ran and played together; Ania's former school was for girls only.

Out of the 40 girls in her former class, only four others had been Jewish, a fact they were always obliged to remember. Every morning, the Polish girls stood and prayed, and the Jewish girls stood silently, waiting for the prayers to be over. A priest came during the week to teach religion; for Ania and her four friends, this was a free hour during which they went out into the playground to play ball or hopscotch.

Ania now stood, embarrassed and apprehensive, at the entrance to her new classroom. But, suddenly, a chubby little girl with long plaits and sparkling eyes got up and said: 'Ania, I saved you a place. Come and sit by me.' This was little Edit, who knew Ania from the Jewish Sports Union, where they both had exercised in the afternoon, until the outbreak of the war. Reli and I saw that someone was looking after our younger sister, so we both went to our own classes.

My first lesson is geography. The teacher is extremely cross-eyed; despite his glasses, he looks at one place and sees another. When he addresses a particular student, saying, 'You there, stand up!' two or three pupils rise and ask: 'Me, sir?'

Since the war began, this teacher seems somehow different, as do the rest of our instructors; it is no longer the same school at all. The teachers try to continue with their regular lesson plans, but we all know that the days of the school are numbered; it is like a tiny boat being tossed by tremendous waves, clearly destined to capsize one day.

Our teachers sadly relate the story of Poland's complete surrender. Warsaw, the last centre of resistance, had fallen after a heroic battle, the city isolated and besieged. Molotov cocktails thrown by starving women and children could not prevail against the German tanks.

Meanwhile, Father is managing our new life at home. He rises on his own early every morning and secures wood and coal to light the stoves. Before our departure for school, we children stand in the long queues waiting for food, sometimes for two hours or more. I get into line while it is still dark out, and when dawn breaks either Reli or Ania comes to switch with me. Mother learns to cook new dishes, using whatever is available. She gives us groats instead of fish, and bakes potato cakes rather than cheesecakes. With a bare teaspoon of sugar, she makes the base for tea, and she begins using cornflour; cornmeal porridge becomes daily fare.

Father still leaves every morning for work, but the business is already out of his hands; a German supervisor is in charge, and my father is now merely one of his employees. Father's business is essential to the Germans, for the supply of trees is diminishing. Father's private railway lines, which until now had allowed him to transfer cargo directly from the trains to his warehouse, are now all loaded with wood. The trains are filled to bursting, then sent off throughout the Reich. During the first few months, the Germans observe the rules of the game, paying my father for the lumber they removed from his warehouses. The beautiful new building on our block, the one covered in black tiles where the Polish academicians had lived, is now the location of the German local government. Once a month, Father sends Ania there, for she is the only one in the family who goes out without wearing the armband, and she receives payment for the wood. The clerks treat her politely, calling her 'Fräulein'.

The Germans now close the Hebrew school. Mother calls the three of us together and asks Reli and me to teach Ania. Halinka, a friend of Ania's, has an older sister, Rina, who is 16. So we, the three oldest, prepare a programme to teach the two youngsters. Rina teaches geography and nature studies, Reli is responsible for Polish, Hebrew and history lessons, and I have to teach mathematics, physics and chemistry. We design a strict, disciplined lesson-plan.

Our pupils complain that Rina's lessons bore them to death. I don't prove much of a teacher, either; only the experiments we attempt during my lessons manage to arouse any interest. But Reli's lessons are truly engaging; she is a born teacher, knowing instinctively how to present a lesson. As a sign of her appreciation, Halinka's mother surprises Reli with a lovely, delicate gold bracelet, an extremely precious gift in those days.

My parents continue to seek some way out, but all the paths are blocked. They write letters abroad, but there is no way of knowing if they reach their destinations. No answers return from any of them. In March 1940, they write to my aunt in Eretz Israel. The letter is cautiously worded, because of the censor, but between the lines is a clear SOS. Father wrote the following:

My dear sister,

It puzzles me that since the war broke out we have heard nothing from you. Hania wrote to you some two months ago, and that letter, too, remains without a reply. There really must be some way to keep in touch, and we want so badly to stay in contact with our relatives, especially with you.

Lately, I've been very worried and depressed, for many reasons, but what weighs on me the most is the uncertainty of the future. Perhaps you could suggest something? Dunek C. sent his brother certain papers; maybe you could ask him, perhaps in the end you can do something to help us. I don't know what the situation is like there, how you're feeling, etc., but I hope all is well with you. In any case, please write and think about what we may be able to arrange.

We're all healthy; I'm out of work, but for now we're getting by. We just have to budget and

conserve very closely. I'm selling the apartment.
We see Mania and the rest of the family fairly
often. The situation is pretty much the same
everywhere.

Yours,
H.

P.S. Send your reply by way of Belgium.

To the same letter, Mother added:

Dearest,

A long time has passed since your last letter. I
can't understand why you don't write. There's so
much to tell...but the most important thing is that
we would love so much to see you all, if somehow
that is possible. Life here goes on. We're all fine; the
children are growing, but they haven't much to
keep them busy – to be more exact, nothing at all.
They study on their own.

I'm asking you from the bottom of my heart:
please write, please try to help us. I've been told that
there's an agricultural school near you, at Ben-
Shemen. I would so love to send our Izio there. We
would very much appreciate it if you could inquire
for him, and perhaps help him to be accepted there.
I hope you won't forget my request, and that you'll
write to us.

This letter, too, like all the others, went unanswered.

One clear morning, a young German woman appeared at our
door with an official notice from the Department of Housing.
So we had to give her a room, and we had no choice but to
move out of ours, the children's room. The three of us now
moved into the attractive family room.

The new tenant is a physical education teacher in a school
for German children under the Occupation regime. She

comes back to her room late each evening, sometimes with a man, or with several. We hear them speaking in German, laughing. Strewn about the shower are her underclothes, and the bathroom is often occupied by strangers. In the morning, Fräulein Paula and Herr Grada irritate one another, especially when both want to use the shower, and they treat each other without even the slightest forms of courtesy, not even speaking in a civil tone of voice.

The room where we now sleep is full of valuable furniture, and also has several original paintings hung on its walls. A grand piano also stands there, for Reli's use alone; she has played since the first grade. But now the piano is only a nuisance, taking up space, and Father finds a Polish family who agree to store it for us; Father is gradually distributing all our valuable property among Polish acquaintances.

In the middle of that winter, Jews are instructed to appear at the offices of the government in order to stamp their special identity cards – the 'Kankarta'. Some of them fail to receive the required stamp, and are sent to work inside the Reich, no-one knows exactly where. They refuse to stamp my card or Reli's. Father learns that a friend of Fräulein Paula's works in the office responsible for stamping the documents; he turns to this German woman for help. She scarcely understands what he is talking about: 'A stamp?' The whole matter seems strange to her, but she promises to try to help.

For now, however, it is dangerous for us to go out in the streets without a stamped identity card; everyone says that a Jew caught with no stamp will surely be killed, and the Germans were never lax in these matters during that period.

Father now rents a room in Bronowitsa, a village adjacent to Cracow, where Reli and I move our lodging and belongings. Before my departure, I manage a last visit to Vladek, who was living in our neighbourhood. He, his parents and sister also have to leave Cracow; they have decided to go to Bochnia.

Vladek was my closest friend; all the best memories of my childhood are linked with him. We played football and ping-pong together, and as a team we played pranks and tricked gullible people on April Fools' Day. We talked constantly, exchanging impressions from the books of Karl May and Jack London; together, we wove elaborate, long-term plans for the future. Among these dreams we found ourselves in the wilderness of the Apaches, or wandering the unknown lands of Mars or the moon.

Vladek was blond, with delicate features, and nearly a head shorter than me; he was always trying in vain to stretch up to my height. Yet even as he grew, I grew at the same rate. His parents claimed that books were the cause of his small stature, that he read too much late at night and his body suffered from lack of sleep.

As I arrive at their home now, I find them in the process of packing, getting ready to leave. They are all despondent, leaving their flat, not knowing when they will return.

'Strong and brave!' I urge Vladek, our own private slogan.

'Strong and brave,' he answers, and we both know how much lies behind these three words: a shared vow that nothing will ever break our friendship, that we will meet after the war, to continue to build on our plans – and also fulfil them.

The winter which Reli and I spent in Bronowitsa was both cold and snow-filled. A heavy, white blanket covered our village; all was a radiant white as far as the eye could see, the trees and rooftops, literally everything. Clearing the snow and moving it from place to place on the orders of the Germans was our only source of income. We returned from the work half-frozen, and tried to warm up with boiling tea instead of the hot meals we could not prepare for lack of coal, wood, or even suitable food.

On the first Friday of our stay in the village, at about 3 p.m., as we are trying to soak up the last warmth from the rays of the setting sun, we suddenly notice in the distance a tiny figure, all alone in the white world. It draws slowly closer, struggling through the deep snow along a path rarely used; we stare, not believing our eyes, and recognize – Ania!

Jumping up and dancing for joy, we run to meet her. She is carrying a large basket in one hand, and in the other a special set of pots designed for the transfer of hot food. Her face is crimson from the cold and the long, strenuous walk.

'My hands, oh, my hands!' she whimpers.

We quickly relieve her of the basket and the pots, hugging and kissing her.

'What's this in your basket, Little Red Riding Hood?'

The basket is indeed full of delights. Mother had worked hard all morning and had prepared everything for the Sabbath, exactly as in better days. She had even baked my favourite chocolate cake; all these delicacies were sent because her heart ached at the thought of the Sabbath her children were forced to celebrate in the village, by themselves.

Ania did not need to be asked twice to make the trip; she was miserable at home without her brother and sister, so she jumped at the chance to bring them home-cooked food and be with them.

'How did you find your way here, Annushia?' we asked in wonder.

'I just kept walking until I got here, that's all. I left the apartment at one, so it only took two hours.'

We went inside our room and sat together on one bed. It never crossed our minds to take off our coats. Reli takes Ania's icy hands and begins to rub them, while I try to entertain her with stories of 'wonders and miracles'.

'This morning I wanted to make an omelette. I take an egg and crack it, and what comes out – a yellow and white ice-ball! I've never seen anything like it! Hey, Ania, look here...'

I begin to whistle, and a column of steam rises out of my mouth, just like that from a teapot.

'See?'

'It's not all that warm at home, either, you know,' Ania puts in. 'Mother and Father moved out of their room, so now we're all in the same room, in order to save fuel. It's running low already, Father says, and the winter has just begun.'

Ania has to start back, for it is a long walk home.

A new problem arose for us. Our landlord began to borrow money from us. The sums were small in the beginning, but increased as time went on. I realized we would have to move before we had 'loaned' him all our money.

The new apartment, which was not easy to find, stood adjacent to the flat of another Jewish family, a fact that pleased us greatly. One day, we had a visitor. A young German soldier, around 19 years old, stood in our doorway, a loaf of army bread in his hand.

'Excuse me, Fräulein, may I?' he stammered, facing Reli.

Reli looked at him, at a loss for words. She had met the soldier the day before, at dusk, on her way back from shopping, with her groceries in her arms. He offered to help her carry her things, and accompanied her to the door of the house. As he left he said: 'See you later, Fräulein.'

We did not really know what to do about him, but he did not wait for an invitation, entering the room and sitting down on one of the chairs. He began to tell us, in short simple sentences, about the village where he had been born, about his parents, brothers and sisters. From time to time he added: 'It's not good, war, not good...'

The young man's unit was stationed in Bronowitsa, and from that day on he began to visit every evening. Each time he brought, instead of flowers, a loaf of bread as a gift for Reli.

Reli made me swear not to be out of the room, not to leave her alone for a minute with the soldier; once I had left for a moment, and the German had tried to kiss her, which frightened her terribly. Things were easier for us when the soldier was transferred to another place. He wrote letters to Reli, in the unrefined hand of a simple villager, saying he hoped to return soon, to see her again, and that he hoped she would be happy to see him, too.

He did in fact come back, a few weeks later, his simple face expressing genuine happiness. The courting was renewed. I knew that I had to speak to him and tell him to stop coming to visit, open his eyes to the underlying danger of the situation, both for us and for himself. To make matters worse, I got a stern lecture from the village butcher's wife, who caught me one day and said: 'You think it's all right that this *Schwab** comes every day to see your sister? Let him look for girls from his own master-race, and leave our daughters alone. We've got enough troubles because of them already. Does your father know about this business? Never mind, I'll see to it that he does.'

It was useless to apologize or make excuses to her, for I knew she was right. *I've just got to talk to that soldier*, I thought; *I'll do it tomorrow*. But the butcher's wife was as good as her word; she reached Father first, telling him everything. He appeared at our apartment the following day, risking the long dangerous walk on his own.

Our visitor turned up a few minutes later. In a quiet, contained voice, Father explained to him that he would have to stop coming to see us. The soldier listened, shocked, and his face registered his incomprehension: *I'm just a country boy*, it said, *and I can't follow your reasoning*.

'But a human being is a human being, what difference does it make what his race, religion, or nationality is?'

He left our apartment hurt and ashamed, and we never saw him again.

Father gave us permission to come home for a visit.

'Be very careful on the way, and come into the apartment by the back stairway up to the kitchen.'

After waiting two days, we set out for the trip back home. We tried our best to walk like everyone else, but we were far from calm; what if they stop us and ask for our papers? By the time we reached the city night had fallen, and the streets were empty of people. It was very still. All of a sudden the sound of steps behind us. Turning around, we saw a small brown puppy, who was matching his paces to ours. We stopped, and he halted, too. We tried to lose him, going into alleys and

* *Schwab*: a derogatory slang term for Germans in general.

around buildings, but he stuck with us.

'He's so sweet,' Reli says, and he looks up at her with friendly eyes and wags his tail, as if he had understood.

'But whose is he?' I wonder.

The dog has a nice collar with a number on it, a sign that he does indeed have owners. We continue on our way, trying in vain to shake him. The puppy just will not be separated from us. We finally give up, and the three of us go on together – Reli, 'Brownie', and me.

Reaching Lobzowska Street, we can already see our apartment in the distance.

'This is is where it's the most dangerous,' I whisper to Reli. 'Just so none of the neighbours see us; there's no shortage of informers.'

We sneak in through the gate and move towards the back steps, which are used to bring in coal, wood, and other supplies. We are pressed up against the wall, hidden from sight. In the courtyard voices are heard, and someone either climbs or descends the front steps. We wait, trembling; Reli puts her finger to her lips, as a sign to the puppy to be still. The dog does not make a sound, as if grasping somehow the seriousness of our situation. When all is quiet again, we proceed towards the kitchen door, crawling on all fours under Herr Grada's window. We finally made it, thank heavens, and Brownie is with us.

Father is very upset that we have brought the dog.

'You don't know what you're doing!' he whispers angrily. 'This dog is liable to bring disaster on our heads. Someone is certain to be looking for him. And if they check closely, they'll be able to follow his tracks in the snow and come here. Who knows, maybe they'll show up in a police jeep? This is just what we needed, really. Throw that dog out of here this minute!'

Reli is in tears. 'He loves me. Maybe he doesn't have anywhere to go, either. I won't let you put him out, poor little thing.'

She strokes his smooth, silky back, and he wriggles all over with pleasure.

Father gives in. The dog receives a bowl of food, and Reli makes him a bed in the kitchen.

The visit goes by without any trouble. We stay there to sleep; five of us crowd into one room and talk in whispers, sitting without light. In the nearby room, Fräulein Paula is enjoying her night-time visitors. At dawn, we again stole away, back to Bronowitsa. Before we set out, however, Ania told us that Stepha had been asking about Reli. She wanted to tell Reli that the 'group' still got together every Friday night to celebrate the Sabbath, and that they all missed her.

'This Friday, they'll all be at Stepha's,' Ania added.

I could feel Reli's longing for her friends; I was also starving for the company of those my own age. Encouraged because the visit home had gone so smoothly, when the sun went down that Friday we made our way through the darkness to Stepha's house. The two-hour walk, by now, was nothing to us; arriving at Stepha's and finding all our friends there, we felt new life flow into us. The meeting was wonderful, and cheered us up tremendously. I saw Reli sitting across the room, grinning with joy; we sang every song that came into our heads, including one in Hebrew:

> There is the cherished land of our fathers,
> Where all our dreams will come true...

We sang many other songs, some whose words we did not understand, yet it did not really matter; words had no meaning, for the meaning lay in our merely being together. We were drunk on the closeness, the sense of good-fellowship.

Stepha's mother served treats; a bowl of pudding for everyone. The pudding was sweet, truly a taste of heaven.

Those moments at Stepha's were very dear to us. We pushed aside the thought that in a little while we would be cut off from everyone, having to slip away under the cover of darkness along the snowy path out of the city, back to the isolation we never deserved. The time with our friends gave us new fortitude, and the bonds of affection could not be broken; they would link us on our way and still later, back in the village. Reli and I both knew this deep inside, no words were needed to say it. The group teased us in high good humour and called us 'the Mutual Admiration Society', meaning me and my two sisters. 'Rather an abnormal situation...', they would joke.

I was in the middle, between the two of them. Little Ania was my favourite playmate, and what is more, a great audience for my imagination and its stories. With Reli only one year older than me, we were like brothers the same age. We were in the same youth movement. Now, in our exile, we walked along, very grateful just to have one another.

Chapter Three

Days, weeks, months passed, the oppression ever worsening. The last sparks of optimism concerning the forecasts about the weakness of the *Blitzkrieg* had long ago been extinguished. All of Europe, except for Great Britain, was in the cruel embrace of the Nazis. Centres of resistance were brutally suppressed. States fell, governments toppled, rivers of blood flowed while homes and bridges were demolished, private and public property looted. The depraved powers of darkness triumphed, rising above and engulfing all in their path, while below was starvation, sickness, certain death. The Jews were trapped, with no way out.

Spring, 1941. The snow began to melt in the feeble rays of the sun, the light spring breezes. On the Wisla River the ice breaks loose, and its waters flow freely again. The trees seem abashed at their nakedness, and begin to cover themselves with the first hints of spring. Choirs of birds announce their return from distant lands. For the birds, freedom; for us, confinement and prison.

In March, 1941, a high wall was erected around several streets in Podgosha, a small quarter on the other side of the Wisla. This wall soon enclosed the Jews of Cracow, along with those of the suburbs and nearby villages, all in the name of the exalted purpose of rendering the entire area *Judenrein* – clean of Jews. For Reli and me, it was a chance to be reunited with our family.

In the Ghetto, we were shoved into an apartment together with three other families; that meant 18 people living in three rooms. I was 16 when I came to live within these walls, in an

area of only a few blocks, the living space for all those human
beings set apart by the Germans in their calculated evil
fashion. Only the sky above the roofs of the crowded
buildings, above the stifling and stale atmosphere, was the
same sky on both sides of the wall.

Reli was 17, I was 16, and Ania was 13$^1/_2$ years old; the
days passed, and we spent the years of our adolescence
within those walls, continuing to study, sing, and dance. Here
were formed the bonds of first love; I had, in my brief youth,
very few hours as beautiful as those I knew with my Lusia.

A boy named David (in my mind I saw him as King David)
and Reli's friend, Esther, fall in love. Esther's parents are
pleased, and take the lone youth into their home as a son.

Reli and Esther opened a kindergarten. The one good
kindergarten, still open when the Ghetto was established,
was the well-known school run by Mrs Mania; it was closed
owing to the sudden death of that wonderful woman, and
many of the children were left neglected. There were even
more children under primary school age who simply
wandered the streets with nothing to do; their parents had no
time to take care of them.

So Reli and Esther close off an area on the edge of the
Ghetto, setting up a covered enclosure and decorating it with
whatever the meagre supplies allow, but putting their whole
hearts into it. The number of children in their school increases
steadily, as they turn the little corner into a comforting shelter
for the young ones. The girls themselves study in the
afternoon with an ex-kindergarten teacher, learning the
methods of instructing and caring for the children. The older
children, including Ania and her friends, study with teachers
who have been dismissed from their positions.

In the summer of 1942, the anxiety in the Ghetto
deepened; everyone was again commanded to have their
papers stamped. As in the first instance, some of the people
did not receive the required stamp on their identity cards. Of
my mother's three brothers, the youngest had fled eastward
at the outbreak of the war, and had not been heard from

since; the other two lived in the Ghetto with their families. Uncle Wolfe and Aunt Adela have three children: Henri, ten years old; Araleh (Aaron), seven; and Ella, five. My aunt and uncle are among those who fail to get the stamp on their papers. With the first 'round-up', they are forced to leave; no-one knows where they are being sent. To resist is out of the question, even to consult on the matter is impossible, for the operation begins without warning – hundreds of loaded guns direct those who are condemned to exile. A rumour spreads that they are being transferred to labour camps. Maybe, it is whispered, the new place is better than the starving, cramped Ghetto, which teems with lice and disease. It is probably better, so they say, for the time being that the little children are not dragged along; the youngsters will stay with their aunt and uncle, and will be sent to their parents after they have settled into their new location. Maybe Uncle Wolfe and Aunt Adela will even be able to come back themselves to fetch their children.

There is no time to think things through, to sit and consider all the options. Araleh and Ella are already in our building, while outside marches the dismal procession of men, women and their families. All have a pack on their backs, or bundles in hand. They walk in fives, and on both sides of them march armed guards. We stand near the window; I am holding Araleh, Ania has Ella. With terrified eyes, we view the scene; there they are, Uncle Wolfe and Aunt Adela, between them the ten-year-old Henri, who carries a knapsack almost as big as he is on his back. We wave to them, throwing kisses. They spot us in the window, but are afraid to make any sort of gesture in return; only their expressions speak, begging us: *Guard our children, please, take care of them* ...

Ella and Araleh remain with us. The brother and sister stay close to one another, sad and withdrawn. In vain we try to amuse them, to cheer them up. There is little food in the flat, but even the small amount we give them they cannot seem to swallow; their tiny throats are tight, and they cannot even speak.

Two weeks later, another group is seized. We had not yet recovered fully from the shock of the first, and now again, more people are taken. This time Uncle Shaike and Aunt Rozia are sent away. They have two sons; Romek, who is nine, and Araleh (another Aaron), aged six. Once again, the same picture: Aunt, Uncle, and Romek on foot, passing by our window, disappearing. The younger boy, little Aaron, stays behind with us, just until they get settled in a bit...

Thus, our family grew from five to nine people. Grandmother (from my mother's side) was now dependent on us, along with the three other children. Araleh, the nine-year-old, was a lovely boy, with delicate features and light, blond hair, straight and smooth as silk. He was very sensitive, and suffered sometimes from earaches. Little Aaron also had blond hair, but his was very curly. With his round face and rosy cheeks, his entire little being radiated beauty and health, both inside and out. Yet little Ella was considered the beauty queen, at least in the opinion of her parents and Grandmother. She was the tiniest figure in the family, the favourite child and truly a delight to her parents, who were dazzled by the happiness she brought them.

After the two round-ups, the area of the Ghetto was decreased, and we had to crowd together even closer. We now lived in a two-room apartment. Each day we all left to do forced labour, only Grandmother, Ania, and the three little ones remaining at home. The housework, securing food, baking bread, preparing meals, as well as the care of the children, all fell on Ania's slim shoulders. The youngsters began to warm towards Ania, getting used to the situation, to the absence of their parents.

A problem arises in trying to care for the thick hair of little Ella. Ania tries her best to avoid having to shave that lovely little head, not to spoil her title as the tiny beauty queen. The smooth blond hair of Araleh and the curly blond locks of little Aaron have already been shaved off; an act which hardly affected their lovely features at all. It was becoming more and more difficult to wash at home, so when I got back from work, I began to take the two boys with me to the public bath, where I washed their bodies with coarse laundry soap.

From time to time, Ania acquires fresh foods like milk, cheese, or eggs – things we have almost forgotten even exist.

'How did you find them? Where?' we all ask in wonder.

'I went outside today.'

'What!'

Ania herself cannot explain how she succeeds in slipping outside the Ghetto walls, in spite of the strict guards of the Jewish police, the OD (*Ordnung Dienst*), and past the Polish and German armed guards as well. The fate of anyone caught trying to escape is well understood; but then, how is it possible to raise young children without ever giving them, at least once in a while, a cup of milk or an egg?

Many of Reli's and my friends are left homeless and alone in the stifling, overcrowded Ghetto after their parents, brothers and sisters are sent away. Ironically, Reli chose to fall in love with a young man in just this difficult situation. His parents and three brothers had been taken in one of the round-ups. In the beginning, he deluded himself that one day he would see them all again. But with time, like most others, he saw that he was mistaken.

I knew him only slightly. He was handsome, truly captivating; there was something very winning about him, and he had great success with the girls. He was known as 'the Lion'. In my eyes, for some reason he just didn't seem right for my sister. There were many tales about his conquests and triumphs with the young women in the Ghetto, some of them probably exaggerated. He was the silent type, taciturn, and his quietness certainly added to his charisma, as well as to the rumours.

At one point in his relationship with Reli, he suddenly underwent a change. He became very serious, full of mystery. Reli of course felt the difference, the aura of secrecy, and wanted to know what was happening to him. He turned aside her inquiries, and the rebuff hurt her. She felt there was a barrier between them, and she could not accept that.

Demanding that he be frank with her, she told him to decide what his relationship with her was to be.

Reli was very sensitive, and she started to wonder, to suspect: some other girl, maybe? Marc, one of Reli's unsuccessful suitors, worked with the Lion. He disclosed that a beautiful blonde woman had come to visit the place where they worked. The Lion became absent-minded, absorbed in himself; he began to miss meetings he had fixed with Reli, and when they saw one another later, forgot to apologize. Though enamoured, Reli found it hard to put up with this situation.

I saw the Lion often, mainly at the public bath. We generally exchanged meaningless pleasantries, though several times it seemed to me that he wanted to tell me something, and then changed his mind. One day, as I was walking in the street with Araleh and little Aaron, I met the Lion. He asked me what we planned to do with the children.

'We're looking for some solution.'

I told Reli about the meeting. She was very excited herself that day, for several strange things had happened to her. She had been taken to work outside the Ghetto, in some sort of army base. She was ordered to clean out an office, and while she was working there, a young man entered – a Jewish boy who had studied with her class. She was certain it was the same boy; he was wearing a German soldier's uniform, and in her surprise at seeing him she almost cried out, but caught herself in time. Reli had then remembered the rumours around the Ghetto about Jews outside who were wandering about disguised as Poles, Ukrainians, or even as German soldiers. Not collaborators, but simply people who sought to save themselves in that fashion.

When she had finished her work, she was accompanied by two guards to a neighbouring camp, on the bank of the Wisla. She was instructed to wait there for the truck which was to take her and the other girls back to the Ghetto. It was still early. The sentries talked, smoking cigarettes. The day was so lovely, and as the sun warmed her Reli forgot for a moment about the war and the Ghetto, listening to the strains of music, beautiful melodies, which escaped from the windows of the army offices. She sat down on the edge of the riverbank and closed her eyes, surrendering her face to the rays of the sun in hopes of perhaps even getting a bit of a suntan. The Lion would like that. Suddenly she sensed that someone was near her. Opening her eyes, she saw a pretty young gypsy girl, dressed in colourful clothes.

'May I predict your future, Miss? Tell your fortune?'

Before Reli had recovered from her surprise, the gypsy had taken her hand and begun to read her palm.

'My dear,' she said, 'I see that you are trapped, caught like a bird in a cage. But don't be disheartened. There will be more bad in your life, but afterwards much good. I see a handsome young man, very handsome indeed ... But be careful, dear, for you have a competitor. Your rival is also very pretty; her name is ...' and she repeated the name of the lovely blonde girl Marc had described as coming to visit the Lion.

'The pretty gypsy told me a lot of other nonsense,' said Reli, 'but nothing important. One thing troubles me now; it may be that this gypsy is also a Jew in disguise.'

Reli told the Lion about the boy from her class whom she had seen dressed in a German uniform. He listened to her, his face becoming stony, closed.

'I don't think he's a collaborator; he's probably only trying to save his own life,' she said.

'There's another possibility,' said the Lion, quietly.

'What possibility?' asked Reli, uncomprehending.

But the Lion was unwilling to talk about it. Reli recounted her meeting with the gypsy, and the things she had said about the beautiful blonde woman. He smiled, and said nothing.

I could see that something was amiss between Reli and the Lion. Things unsaid and unexplained separated them, hurting Reli, causing her to worry. She decided to break off the affair.

'How is the Lion?' I asked Reli, a few days later. 'Why is it we don't see him around here lately?'

'I don't know,' she replied sadly. 'We're no longer together. I told him that I can't be with him if he's hiding things from me, that I don't understand him.'

'And what did he say?'

'He said he hoped someday I would understand.'

Some time after that, Reli came home one day with her face as white as a sheet. She had heard that the Lion had disappeared. For several days now, he had not shown up at work, nor was he to be found at his flat.

I was silent for a long moment. It was easy to see how deeply Reli still felt about the young man, in spite of the fact that they were no longer together. Finally, I said: 'I wonder, Reli, what it was he wanted to say to me that time we met on the street, when he asked about the children, said he might be able to help.'

Reli's eyes filled with tears. 'And what did he mean when he said "I hope you'll understand someday"? I want to understand now – what's happening to him? Where is he?'

We both remembered one evening, when we were all gathered in our 'clubhouse' to light candles for Hanukka, that he had said, half serious and half in jest: 'We, all the young, must stand up now and fight, like the Maccabees.'

An argument broke out; some said that it was not at all the same set of circumstances, that we were all tied to families, and that it was impossible to fight empty-handed.

'True,' the Lion had replied, 'you all still have something to lose. You have parents, brothers, sisters. It's true that to those who are alone, the desperate ones, it's much easier to be a hero.'

We tried to find out where the Lion was, but it was as if a conspiracy of silence surrounded his disappearance. Only vague hints were given about the dangerous route by which he had escaped. We were also told that for some things silence was the best policy, because anyone even suspected of being in touch with the underground was dealt with brutally.

We heard no more about him until a few months later. One day we were told that he had succeeded in being taken into the

Polish underground (it was generally known that the resistance
fighters rarely accepted Jews on equal terms into their ranks),
had been on several operations, then was caught by the
Germans and shot. We did not want to speculate as to how he
was captured and executed. I felt sorry that I hadn't got to know
him better, that he had not included me in his secrets, not taken
me into his confidence. And now – it was over. I did not speak
with Reli about him. I simply could not find the words.

The Ghetto grew steadily worse, the streets filled with people
dressed in rags, beggars and the sick. But then, out of the
blue, came an extraordinary figure, passing by as if sailing.
This was Wuska, the young and courageous wife of Dolek
Liebeskind.* She goes around in a lovely dark blue coat,
edged in lace. The coat must have been made for some joyous
occasion; today, there was no reason to save it. But she kept it,
carrying her head proudly, her pretty face framed by carefully
arranged braids.

Ania, too, had a serious suitor, one of my best friends. His
father, a chemist, and his mother, a pharmacist, had both been
taken away in one of the round-ups. He was only a boy, really,
and now left completely alone in the world. He resolved to
escape to the nearby forest, where there were partisans, both
Polish and Jewish. While not everyone was awarded a
weapon, nevertheless you had a chance there at least, the
opportunity to defend yourself.

The boy appeared one day and asked my father's
permission to take Ania with him to the forest.

'I heard that there are girls among the partisans too,' he
stated, 'and I . . . I'll defend her.'

This brave and frank young man impressed my father
greatly. But he smiled sadly and replied: 'But Ania's occupied
here. She has three little children to care for. What will
happen to them if she goes?'

---

* Dolek Liebeskind: the leader of the Jewish underground in Cracow Ghetto. He
was caught with several others and shot by the Germans. Wuska lives today in
Israel.

The boy escaped from the Ghetto, and we heard nothing more about him, or about the others like him who ran away.

Stepha, Reli's best friend, joins us in the room which already houses twelve people. She too is now on her own, the last of her large family remaining in the Ghetto. Stepha is a very sensible girl, blessed with unusual poise and a fine sense of humour. Her presence has a good effect on all of us, but it is difficult to feed so many mouths. The children suffer the most.

Rumour has it that the Germans are preparing to demolish the Ghetto, after transferring the remaining residents to work camps. New round-ups are in the air; it is said that the weak will be taken first – meaning, of course, the elderly and the children. Father has an idea: maybe Mrs Maus can help; we must reach her and talk with her.

For many years, we had been on good terms with our neighbour, Mrs Maus. She was a German woman who had converted to Judaism after, or perhaps before, marrying a Jew. She then left Germany and settled in Cracow. She observed strictly the laws and traditions of Judaism, kept a kosher kitchen, lit candles on the Sabbath. The Mauses' son, Fredric, studied in the Hebrew grammar school. They gave their daughter the Hebrew name Rute; before the war, she had been Ania's closest friend. Even when the two girls were still infants, the mothers used to go out together to the park and sit on the benches to chat, knit or crochet, while the little girls played hopscotch, tag, or with their dolls.

With the outbreak of the war, Mr Maus and his son went east, and were now in Russian territory. Mrs Maus and Rute (Rutka) remained in Cracow. Along with the Occupation soldiers came Mrs Maus's brother, a member of the SS forces. Father held on to a slim hope that maybe through Mrs Maus and her brother it would be possible to save at least the children. Mother and Father consult on the matter. They tell themselves that even the SS officers have children, which is true enough, and therefore perhaps they will be willing to understand. It is just not conceivable that they are all so...and besides, we've known Mrs Maus for such a long time.

Once again the mission falls on Ania. By routes only she knew, Ania steals out of the Ghetto and walks towards the Mauses' apartment, which she knows so well. She returns later, without good tidings.

'She barely spoke to me,' related Ania. 'When she opened the door and saw me, she went very pale. In a whisper, she told me to go away, not to come in, so that Rutka wouldn't even see me. She said her brother was very cruel even to them, and he threatened that if they were in contact with Jews in any way, he would personally kill them. I didn't accomplish anything,' she apologized. 'I wanted to enter the convent and speak with the nuns, but near the gate was a priest, and he said it was prohibited, absolutely forbidden to go into the convent.'

It was at that point that the plan to buy us false papers was born. According to Father's calculations, I would leave first, and after would come Ania. Everyone agreed that we looked like Slavs, so we would try to find a suitable place to bring the three children. Maybe even some sort of monastery, despite everything. And perhaps my lovely mother, with her light hair and blue eyes, would be accepted as a nun, until the end of the war. For it must end someday, this cursed war...

Father bought us the forged identity cards. My name on the card is Yurek Kowalik, and Ania is named Anna Waletska. Father was advised to send us to a large city where no-one knows us, so that none of our former acquaintances would meet us on the street and perhaps inform on us.

At that time, eastern Poland was under Nazi control, with Lithuania, Latvia and Estonia also conquered. Massive battles were going on somewhere within the huge area of Russia. A dreadful thought haunted us: was there left in the world any power which could stop the Nazi monster? Every place that was occupied became a hell for the Jews, a prison in which they were condemned to death. No-one stood up to defend the Jews, no-one felt any solidarity with the Polish 'sons of Moses'. On the contrary, informers abounded.

Father thought that the city of Lvov would be a safe shelter for us. In exchange for an immense sum of money, he acquires the identity cards, and contacts the Polish underground, as well as a man named Hans Miller. This Miller, it was said, could do almost anything, all doors seemed to open for him, and to be under his wing was to be safe, secure. Father receives a promise that Miller will arrange to get a room for us in Lvov, as well as help us along our first steps in the new city. Through Ledwon, a member of the Polish underground in Cracow, we received the address of the pharmacist, Stanowski, who agrees to function as our mail drop in Lvov.

I arrived in Lvov ten days before Ania. It turns out that after I left, a terrible confusion gripped everyone; the shady connections, the uncertainty as to what was happening to me, worried my parents almost to their wits' end. As the day for Ania's departure drew closer, their doubts increased as to whether they had chosen the right course. But the state of affairs inside the Ghetto was no more encouraging, not at all. In October, the Germans broke into the Ghetto, parading their victims with barbaric cruelty. From the streets and houses, from hiding-places and sickbeds, people were taken and transferred to Appelplatz. Again, no-one deluded himself as to the fate of those sent away.

Fearing that they would take Ania and the children, my parents concealed them in a compartment, one metre square, behind the false wall in a cupboard. In the same tiny room were crowded four other tenants of the apartment: two women, one of them elderly, whose identity cards were unstamped, one short man, almost a dwarf, and our grandmother. Because no-one knew how long they would have to stay in the compartment, they were given a pail in which to fulfil their bodily needs. The little boy, so frightened that he was stricken with an attack of diarrhoea, used the pail almost constantly. Ania related that she and the three children sat together, if it could be called sitting, clinging to one another like a single unit, and took up only half a square metre. They sat thus, in the darkness and stench, without making a sound. The time seemed an eternity. Outside, they could hear wailing, bellows and shouts. It was a nightmare beyond description.

After that same cruel round-up, our parents' fears about Ania's leaving were lessened.

Chapter Four

On the day Father had arranged, Ania put on her school uniform, even taking her bookbag with her. Father and Reli had, in stages, smuggled her luggage to where they were working. Ania left the Ghetto with a group of workers, again succeeding in slipping outside. Beyond the walls, she broke away from the crowd when the sentry wasn't looking for an instant – and suddenly she was free, walking the streets like anyone else. She moved quickly away from the area of the Ghetto, following Father's instructions to go to the apartment of Mrs Appel. This woman, like Mrs Maus, was German, and had married a Pole, who brought her with him to live in Cracow. For many years she was a neighbour of one of our aunts, and became good friends with her. With the occupation of Cracow, Mrs Appel's father arrived at her flat; he was not in uniform, but simply an elderly German citizen.

Ania knocks at the door, and Mrs Appel answers it, smiling and kind; she immediately leads Ania inside. On the kitchen counter rest two elegant vases. Ania recognizes them instantly – they were ours, from our old flat. Mrs Appel follows the young girl's gaze.

'Don't worry, my dear. They're in good hands. We'll return them when we can.'

In the hallway rest our huge basket and Ania's small suitcase, ready for the journey. Mrs Appel's father, a thin man with an impressive moustache, speaks no Polish. He is friendly to Ania, and asks his daughter to translate what he says. He tells her that Father directed that Ania was to take the large basket to Lvov; it contains many valuables which she and her brother could sell if in need of money. Ania cannot grasp fully all they are telling her; she feels as if it is all a dream, or perhaps that it is another girl entirely, not her at all, who stands in the middle of the room dressed in a blue coat and hat, at a loss what to do. Mrs Appel's father takes from the lapel of his coat a round pin with a swastika on it. He asks his daughter to explain: just to be on the safe side, to make a good impression, and he pins it back on his coat.

They order a large coach with a driver and a porter, then bring down the basket and suitcase, Ania following the old gentleman. Mrs Appel kisses her before she leaves; in the coach, her father gives Ania a piece of candy.

The station is changed drastically from what it was in the days we used to leave from there for holidays. It is jammed with people, and filled with an atmosphere of fright and nervousness – *or maybe that's just my imagination*, Ania thinks to herself. The old man buys her a ticket to Lvov, third-class; there would be safety in the anonymity of the large numbers of passengers in this crowded section. Peasant women clamber up into the car, with large shawls covering both themselves and the great sacks on their backs. Only thin strips of their faces are visible under these shawls, which cover their whole body.

People hurry to find a seat. Mrs Appel's father pushes rudely through the villagers, saying in German: *'Platz machen!'* ('Make room, there! Make room!') The harsh German and the swastika on his coat have the desired effect. The passengers move aside, and the old man pulls Ania behind him, finally seating her in the best possible place, next to the window. He explains in gestures that she must not budge from that seat, not give it to anyone. He then descends and sees to it that her basket is lifted onto the train, and left in the passageway. People immediately sit down on it, but Mrs Appel's father motions to Ania that it doesn't matter, it is better that way. Her suitcase he puts up above, on the luggage rack. A whistle sounds; the train is leaving in one minute. The old gentleman puts his hand kindly on Ania's shoulder and says: *'Mit Gottes Hilfe.'* ('With God's help.') He then climbs down from the train.

'It was a long trip,' relates Ania, 'for it wasn't an express train.' There were numerous stops. Villagers and peasants got on or off at the various towns along the way. Across from Ania sat a man in a grey coat, the same man who later helped us to take the basket off the train. Ania saw that the man was wondering about her, that something was puzzling him. He asked her several questions. She blushed with each reply, yet the man smiled at her and said: 'My little Sofie is also shy, like you.' He continued to grin, taking out a picture and showing it to her. When his attention wandered for a few minutes, she pretended to be dozing, so that he would leave her to herself.

The ticket check passed without incident.

'And here I am,' Ania concluded.

We were sitting on a bench in one of the city parks. Since morning, we had been roaming from one park to the next, one avenue after another, sitting a while, then getting up and moving to different spot, as much to warm ourselves as to change places.

'Let's see what Father and Mother gave us,' Ania suddenly suggests.

Pulling a small napkin out of her pocket, she extracts from it a small bun. From inside the roll she pulls out a diamond ring, Mother's ring; the large, well-cut diamond sparkles, truly dazzling, and its points of light blind me, filling me with sweet memories.

'How did you get it?' I ask. 'I thought they had handed it over long ago.'

Before the war, the ring was never off my mother's finger. It had been simply part of her left hand. When the Germans came, the ring vanished from her finger, and I had been certain that it was lost or confiscated long before now.

'Father managed to keep it, God only knows how. He gave it to me yesterday, telling us to take care of it. He said he believed that it, the ring, would care for us, too. He asked us not to give it up, ever, unless there was no other choice; if surrendering it could save our life, then we should give it up. He wants you to hold on to it, because... well, you're older, and also... also, you're in the greatest danger...' These last words she spoke with great difficulty.

I take the ring from her, put it quickly back into the roll and wrap it in the napkin, slipping it into the pocket of my trousers. May it protect us both, someday, somehow...

Now it is my turn to talk. I tell Ania about Hans Miller and Maximilian, about the pharmacist, Stanowski, and also about Wanda and Kazik.

'I'm going to Kazik's today, too. I think we'll be able to get along well with their help. I would really like to get away from this Hans Miller and the uncertainty of the living situation he's arranged for us. I've got to find work to support the two of us, and then look for another room.'

'Until then', Ania puts in, 'we can sell things from the basket. A nice Gentile lady has agreed to store the stock from Grandmother's store; all sorts of things made from wool, you know: earmuffs, caps, woollen mittens. There's sure to be a demand for those things now, with winter starting.'

Dealing in handicrafts is not exactly my idea of an ideal occupation, I thought to myself; *but at this stage, who can afford to be choosy?* So I said: 'Good, then. Tomorrow we'll get to work, because we really do need some money.'

Ania and I arranged a schedule, deciding not to stay too close to one another, and to meet for only one meal each day, always at a different restaurant.

The following day, I entered a small woollen goods store. I showed the woman behind the counter two of the things Ania had brought in the basket. The woman liked them very much, and asked if she would be able to get more of the same merchandise, in larger quantities. We agreed on a price, and I asked if she had any objection to receiving the goods by mail, directly to her store, and then paying for them later. She consented, made up an order, and I promised to take care of the shipping.

Ania met with similar success in another store. Through

Stanowski, we sent Father the addresses of the two stores, as well as the orders. The packages arrived a few days later; we recieved a notice that the goods had been sent, and promptly went to collect the money.

That same day was 10 November, Ania's fifteenth birthday. I had completely forgotten, and she paid no attention to it either; or perhaps she just put up a good front. At home, we had always celebrated Ania's birthday with a delicious chocolate cake, home-baked, with raisins and almonds, and presents of course... such an occasion was Ania's birthday that Reli and I complained of discrimination in the house, favouring the youngest. And this year, I forgot – but at home, they did not.

When Ania went into 'her' store, that day, the saleswoman told her: 'A package arrived for you, young lady. May I open it?'

'Of course,' Ania replied. 'It's probably the gloves and sweaters you requested.'

The woman opened the package, and indeed, there were inside it the woollen goods she had ordered. There was, however, also a small package among the other things, wrapped in pretty paper and tied with a ribbon. How had Father ever managed it? On the paper was written 'To Ania'.

With trembling hands, Ania opened the small parcel. It was a lovely little powder compact inside a case lined in pink cotton wool, and there was a note in Father's handwriting: 'To my little sweetheart, on her birthday.'

The saleswoman's eyes widened. She had not seen such a beautiful item for some time.

Ania opens the compact and looks in the tiny mirror; her eyes return her gaze, swimming in tears.

'You have quite an admirer there, my girl,' said the surprised woman.

'That's true, very true... quite an admirer,' replies Ania, swallowing her tears. 'May I please have the money for these things?' she continues, shyly.

'Oh yes, of course.' The woman paid Ania, pleased with

the bargain she had made.

Ania related all this to me that evening. We decided to go to a cinema, partly to find a relatively safe and warm place to sit, and also because it was her birthday and we wanted to celebrate.

'How was it at Kazik's today?' she inquired.

'Nice, as usual. There were a million copies to be made. I learned how to peck away on a typewriter a bit.'

'That's good; Father always said that anything you could learn may come in useful someday.'

We fell silent. I knew Ania would have liked to come with me to Kazik's, that it would be so much more pleasant for her than wandering alone around the city. In spite of this, I kept putting off her visit to the Gronowskis from day to day. I liked the young couple extremely, but I was still not sure how far I could trust them. I was afraid that if they saw Ania they would notice the family resemblance between us, or that our tongues would betray us, and that this might cause us some problems. I guess I was simply following Hans Miller's advice, when he told us over and over again: 'It's best that everyone be on his own. In our situation, we're better off alone than together.'

I also continued to delay my registration at the Work Office and the Department of Housing. I knew how hard this was on Ania, how uncomfortable she was in the Bema Street flat, without even the minimum conveniences, no corner for herself, for her own personal care. She dressed and undressed while in bed, under the blankets, embarrassed by the presence of the men, but unable to demand that they look away. Her plight was worsened by the fact that she had no way to take a bath, or to wash her clothes. I racked my brains for a solution to this sorry state of affairs. Ania herself raised the idea of finding a regular job which also offered residence.

'Why not?' she argued. 'I know how to cook and bake pretty well. I did it for our family, so I'm sure I could for other people. And I've also taken care of children before.'

'I don't want you working for strangers,' I tried to object, but the idea actually didn't seem a bad one. Besides, did I have anything better to suggest?

'We can find a family with small children who need help around the house. I'll get along fine, and the most important thing is I'll be out of this awful room.'

So we bought a paper and began looking through the advertisements. Under 'Help Wanted', we found an offer which looked promising:

> Wanted: Girl to care for two children, four and five years old. Preferably live-in. Also some help with housework. Those interested please come to the following address...from the hours of...

Ania was enthusiastic. 'I've got a feeling this is just right for me. I'll go there today.'

'You could look a little longer, or we could buy another newspaper, wait another day or two.'

'Why should I wait? It will be easier for you too if this works out. You'll be able to work more often with Kazik, and maybe then he'll help you find somewhere else to live.'

'The problem with Kazik is that the work at his house is for no salary, and I still haven't told him that I'm not on the official list of residents, nor does he know I'm having problems finding a job and a place to live.'

'You see; one of us simply has to make a start. So I'll try.'

Next morning, Ania set out. I had found in the same paper the address of a carpentry shop looking for apprentice carpenters. I knew about as much about carpentry as I did about astronomy, maybe even less; I had always been interested in the stars. But among the various trades I had always felt the closest identification with carpentry. Maybe because of the material the carpenter works with; I was no stranger to wood. I always felt somehow tied to wood, for it was part of my father's individual make-up.

How many stories I could tell about wood! Each board had its own wonderful tale to unfold; it could tell of its glorious past, when it was part of a living, growing tree in some dense forest, or standing young and alive in some new, burgeoning grove. Father understood the differences between the various sorts of wood even when they were still trees in the forest; he could discern their ages and characteristics, and he knew how to choose between a strong, healthy tree and one that was sick or weak. He used to tell us tales of his hikes through the dense forests, bringing all of us closer to his business, his lifelong interest.

We loved the forest for all its fabulous treasures, for its cool air and fragrance. We learned with Father to distinguish between different species of trees, and came to know the other vegetation in the forest as well; the soft moss at the foot of the trees, the carpet of falling pine needles, the pine cones, and the mushrooms which popped up after the rains. We also loved the round, tiny berries, like small black-red beads, which tasted so tart and sweet.

Then the trees found their new form: boards, piled high in clean, orderly stacks in Father's warehouse. What wonderful hours we enjoyed as children, playing hide-and-seek amid that special, pleasing aroma of wood and resin!

As I entered the small carpentry shop, that old familiar wood-smell surrounded me, with all its memories. The carpenter, sporting a large moustache, stood sawing a board. It was warm and pleasant there. I told him I was looking for work, and he answered that he was seeking an apprentice, for it was hard for him to do all the work by himself.

'Great,' I said. 'I'll be able to start right away.'

'All right, you can work today as a trial.'

I took off my coat immediately and began to roll up my sleeves. The carpenter raised his head from his work, and said:

'But those aren't work clothes you're wearing, my boy; to tell the truth, you don't look at all like a worker to me.'

'I'm a good worker, and I'll prove it to you,' I said. 'I'll come in work clothes tomorrow (*Where will I find them?*). It's a shame to waste time running back home to change, and I'm not worried about these clothes, anyway.'

The carpenter glanced at himself and then at me, at his hands and mine, but before he could begin I caught him and said: 'Listen, sir, I've never worked in this trade before. I had to leave my studies at school because...well, my father died, and...I have to help support my family.'

I'm sure I blushed terribly as I told this pitiful lie.

'Well, all right,' said the carpenter, reconciled. 'It doesn't make any difference to me if you work like that.'

He instructed me to gather up the wood scraps and shavings into a large basket, then take them out into the yard and transfer them into sacks.

I set vigorously to work.

While I was working, I met three or four cats which cavorted around the workshop, and I began to see my new employer was a true cat-lover. The cats didn't do anything, just lay around enjoying themselves or playing with one another, and the carpenter talked to them constantly. One he would scold, another he petted, repeatedly berating and caressing them.

After three hours had passed, he called a break, lighting a small stove and putting a pot of soup on it. When it was hot, he gave me some. To the cats he portioned out milk mixed with water.

'The war...' he seemed to try to explain to them, probably not for the first time. 'War, my friends, and there's not much milk. We have to make do with what's available...'

'Meow, meow...' answered the cats in unison, more than happy with their lot.

What do they care about the war, these cats? I thought, bitterly; *they don't have to hide themselves, or lie. Certainly no-one ever asks them where they're from, or requests their papers.*

The carpenter, as if reading my mind, said in an offhand manner: 'You'll have to bring me a note from the Work Office. It's forbidden to employ people who aren't registered.'

Well, here we go, I thought, and said aloud: 'Of course I'll bring it, sir, there's no problem with that.'

At 4 p.m., I finished work for the day. The carpenter

reminded me to go to the Office. When I brought him the note, he said, we would talk about the duties of the job, and my salary would also include this first day at work.

I went back to the room. I had hoped to find Ania there, to tell her about the day at the carpentry shop, and to hear how her day had gone. To my disappointment, she was not there. My entire body ached from the new work it was not accustomed to. I left the apartment for the market, to buy a little food. I guessed Ania would also be hungry and tired when she returned, and it would be good to make a little 'home-made' dinner for us.

There were few shoppers left at the market; the vendors had begun closing up their stalls. I nevertheless managed to obtain half a loaf of round bread, an onion, a turnip, and some pumpkin jam. I returned to the flat with this booty. Ania had still not returned. I asked the old couple if she had left any message for me.

'She didn't leave a message,' they said, 'but during the day she came back here, took a few of her things, and then left again.'

I relaxed a bit. She must have found a live-in position as she had wanted, or she would not have taken some of her possessions. I felt a bit let down that she had not waited for me to tell me about the people she had met during the day, whom she was going to live with and work for. Why had she not waited for me? Why had she gone off in such a hurry? Maybe it was not a job at all...maybe she...but, no, after all, she had been here and taken some of her things.

When Hans returned, he asked about Ania's whereabouts, if something had happened to her.

'It's OK. She found work,' I answered.

'Be very careful, you two,' he cautioned. 'The Work Office checks carefully, and they always discover forged identity cards. You can't go to the Work Office for any reason; it's absolutely essential to avoid all official places.'

I sank into a deep depression. If what he said was true,

then I had made no progress at all, I had only deluded myself that I had a place to work.

The room was lonely, without Ania. I didn't know what to do. Should I return to the carpenter without a note? Yet he told me explicitly that he would not pay me until he had the official reference of the Work Office.

In the morning, despite Hans's warning, I went to the Work Office, but then I quickly fled, stricken with fear. Many uniformed men were inside the office, and people looking for work. I was sure that a good number of detectives in civilian clothes were also mixing with the crowd, and they were the most dangerous of all. *No*, I thought, *I won't make their job any easier; they won't see me in the Work Office.* Until noon, I meandered through the city aimlessly. By the afternoon I found myself near Kazik's home, and decided to go up to see him. Fortunately, he and Wanda were at home. My reception was warm, as usual, yet during the two weeks which had passed since I first met them, a certain small but fixed distance between us had not lessened. Kazik filled me in on the latest news.

'In the Ghetto in our city, the situation is deteriorating. The rumour is that in these next few days there will be a large round-up. They're moving the Jews to Yanowska camp – one of the worst ones.'

This was the first time Kazik had mentioned in my presence the Ghetto, or the Jews. His face was very grave, and his forehead suddenly furrowed. I remained quiet, but everything inside me was crying out:

Kazik, why are you doing nothing? We've got to stop the round-ups... it's just inconceivable that there's nothing we can do to help...

But my throat was dry, my jaw clenched. Kazik also sat silently, and our eyes avoided each other.

Wanda came in, setting cups of tea before us.

'Why so grim, my dears? Why, the Germans are falling like flies... [she meant in the battle for Stalingrad] they'll end up just like Napoleon's armies; they'll soon learn about the

Russian winter. I'm sure their end will be terrible and bitter.'

'Yes, but until then...' murmured Kazik.

Wanda just sighed.

'Katya, my sister-in-law, is coming in a little while.'

I made a movement as if to get up and leave. Up to this point, I had met no-one in the Gronowskis' apartment but themselves. I thought perhaps they would not want me to be there with other people.

'No, no, you're not disturbing anything!' Wanda stopped me. 'You can sit in the small room with Kazik's desk and go over yesterday's reports. We have no secrets from Katya. Her husband, my brother, was murdered by the Germans almost immediately on their entrance into Lvov, due to his active resistance. She's so young, and already a widow, with her little, fatherless children. But she's also very brave; she's sure there will come a day when her children will be proud of their father.'

'How old are Katya's children?' I inquired, with a strange feeling that the ages of this unknown woman's children were somehow important to me.

'Little Yadzia is five, and Yatsek is only four,' replied Wanda. 'Nice little children, but very sensitive after their father's death, especially because Katya is often out of the house; she started teaching again, her profession before marriage. She has to support her family now.'

'And who takes care of the children?'

Wanda looked at me in surprise, as if trying to fathom my sudden interest in Katya and her children.

'Mother, my mother and also the late Stephan's, lives with them; but she's no longer young and it's hard for her to run the house and take care of the children, too.'

The doorbell rang. Wanda led me to the nearby room, and I sat down at Kazik's desk.

'Here,' she said, handing me a stack of typed pages, 'this is the latest report, to read in the meantime.'

The door between the two rooms remained ajar, and I heard Wanda and Kazik greet their sister-in-law in their typically warmhearted fashion.

'Wanda! Kazik!' I heard the guest's agitated voice, 'I came because I have to talk to you – I think we've all lost the last traces of humanity.'

'Katya, dear! Calm down, tell us what happened. Is there something the matter with the children?'

'They're such difficult children, they need so much attention ... and one of them always seems to be ill. But that's not the problem today.'

'So tell us, what is it?'

'You remember that I put an ad in the paper for someone to care for the children. I told you ... '

My heart stopped, and my body went rigid, as I listened tensely to what followed.

'Yesterday morning, a nice young blonde girl appeared at the door in answer to the ad. I was just hurrying off to work ... '

Now I knew that the eerie feeling which had gripped me when Wanda spoke to me about her sister-in-law and her children was not without a basis. What an incredible coincidence!

'The boys were upset, and fighting over one of their toys. The girl said she knew how to take care of children, and was ready to help with the housework. She said she could start immediately. I wanted to make it easier for Mother, so I agreed. The girl sounded very nice; I asked her what her name was, and she replied: "Ania, they call me Ania."

'So I told her she could stay. I said: "The first thing is to dress the boys and take them out for a walk. Just keep an eye on them, for they're very sensitive to the cold, and don't take them near the busy streets – they're both very mischievous. Mother will show you where their clothes are, and everything else. If you have any questions, ask her. I must run off to work. Good luck, Ania."

'She wanted to know if she could leave later for an hour, to bring her belongings to our apartment. "Of course," I said. "Mother will show you where you can put your things, and where you'll sleep." Then I left for school.

'When I came home, Ania was sitting in the kitchen, peeling potatoes. On seeing me she smiled, but I felt that the smile cost her a lot of effort. I asked Mother how she got along with the children. Mother seemed to hedge before answering: "It takes children time to get used to a stranger, and she herself isn't much more than a child, I'm sure she's no more than fifteen. She's quick and knows how to work, but she ... she's not from a simple home, and she's a bit flustered. I gave her something to eat, and it seemed to stick in her throat."

'After I had listened to Mother,' continued Katya, 'I went to Ania and asked where she had walked with the boys. I instantly sensed that she was not from our city. "Are you from Lvov?" I inquired. "No," she replied quietly. "Then why did you come here to work?" "I needed the money, and a place to stay. I'm also willing to work for no salary."

'Then I understood. I could feel how each question was painful to her, and I realized that the girl was trying to hide her race, as if it were some horrible disgrace. You see now, Wanda, Kazik? I didn't ask her any more questions; there was no need to – I knew the crime she was trying to conceal was the fact that she was born of Jewish parents.

'Stephan's mother wouldn't speak to me all day. That night, Ania tried to put the children to bed. They wanted nothing to do with her, wanted only me; naturally enough, for they were not accustomed to her. When she saw that I was with the boys, she went into the kitchen to do the dishes. Later on, she asked if she might use the bathtub. "By all means," I said. She had a bath, and then went to bed.

'I didn't sleep the whole night. In the morning I called Adam, you know, my friend and counsellor since Stephan's death. I asked him urgently to come over, and informed the school that I couldn't be there for the first few hours. Adam came, and I told him the entire story, and that I was frightened. I expected him to say something like: "Katya, aren't you ashamed! You, whose husband was killed for his resistance to all this cruelty. Be brave, Katya! Be human!"

'Instead, Adam told me that I must not do this, that I should remember that a death sentence awaits those who hide Jews. He said that it's enough that Stephan is gone, now I must think only of my children.

'We called Ania and I explained to her that our lives were in danger if she stayed with us. The young girl stood erect, without making a sound. I feel so angry with her, just furious – why didn't she simply ask to stay, to be saved? Maybe then ... I don't know, maybe I would have changed my mind. If she had at least said: "Wherever did you get the notion that I was Jewish? I'm not at all Jewish," I might have accepted the lie and taken the chance. But all she said was that she understood that we couldn't endanger ourselves, that our lives and the lives of the children were more important, and she didn't want us to get into trouble because of her. She gathered up her things, thanked me for the meals she had eaten, and for the shower, then walked out. Tell me, are we even human beings any more?'

Katya sobbed softly; Wanda and Kazik made no attempt to comfort her. After a short while, she asked: 'Have you heard any news lately?'

'The Germans still have an enormous military advantage.'

'What are they doing with the Jews, where are they sending these poor people?'

After a long pause, Kazik answered: 'The Germans have established camps in Germany, also in the other occupied countries, and in our own country. They're called "concentration camps", but they are simply death camps; the Nazis are killing thousands of Jews there every hour, with the most advanced technological methods.'

'And we're silent, Kazik? What do our leaders in London tell us? What do they say we should do?'

'They don't discuss the matter.' There was pain in Kazik's voice. 'They're sitting in a safe place, far from the blood and murder. They keep telling us to be strong.'

The conversation turned aside to the exiled leaders, to the

food rationing, fuel supplies, the approaching cold of winter. The Jews being put to death, thousands each hour, are once again forgotten.

Katya is in a hurry to get back home, so she takes her leave and goes out. Wanda and Kazik promise to visit her.

I struggle to control the turmoil within me. After Katya's departure, I turned to Kazik with questions concerning the report. I did not touch on any of the issues really important to me. I am still not sure if I did the right thing, if I did not make a mistake in avoiding the one subject so painful and close to me.

That evening, I parted with my hosts a little earlier than usual; I rose and left. After hearing what Ania had been through in the last two days, I wanted to be with her, to encourage her and let her know that not everyone in the world was turning their back on her, like a stranger. For I would be there, next to her, with her come what may. I literally ran through the streets.

I reach the flat, breathing heavily, and there is Ania, very quiet, her small suitcase resting on the large basket.

'Hello, Ania. I was worried about you.'

'Hello, Yur.'

What can I possibly say to her? I thought – *but then, she doesn't realize that I know.*

Ania began before I could.

'You know, that job didn't work out. Those children – they just didn't want me to take care of them. For Araleh, little Aaron, and Ella, I'm the right person; for those two little boys, I'm not. I miss them so much, little Aaron and Ella, my Araleh. I just can't stand it any more, I want to go home.'

Ania's lips were quivering, she was on the verge of tears.

'We don't have a home, Annushia...you know that very well. It's all destroyed. There's nowhere to return to. We've got to survive here.'

Ania then smiled at me, as if ashamed at the attack of weakness she had displayed.

'I sold a few hats today for a good price,' she said, in a happier tone. 'They were from the basket, because my store did not receive its weekly package. What about at your store? Did their orders come in?'

'No, nothing came in there this week, either. We'll see, maybe in another few days.'

'You know, I almost got killed today. When I left the flat where I stayed last night, I caught the trolley bus. In one hand I had my suitcase, and in the other my wallet with my money and identity card. As I got off, I suddenly noticed that all I had was my suitcase. I had left my wallet on the trolley bus! I was so frightened at being without the one document, *the* identity card, afraid that I would have to notify the police, or that someone would find it and then they would start looking for me. I ran like a maniac after the trolley bus and jumped onto it, still with my suitcase in my hand, when the bus was already moving pretty fast. People helped pull me inside, but they were angry, asking me if maybe I'd just got tired of being alive. I was overjoyed when I found the wallet, which nobody had touched. At the next stop I got off and walked all the way back on foot. But that's not important; the main thing is that I've still got my identity card.

'What have you been doing these last two days?' she finally asked me.

I recounted to her all about the day with the carpenter, the cats, about what Hans had said and how I had passed by the Work Office, as well as some of the story about the morning at Kazik's. I did not mention Katya's visit, or the tale I had chanced to hear.

Hans returned, saying that in the Ghetto the situation was getting steadily worse.

'It looks as if they're going to tear down the Ghetto. They're planning a big round-up,' he said. 'The people will be transferred to Yanowska, and from there...who knows?'

Hans's story resembled very closely what I had heard at the Gronowskis'.

Ania sat, dejected, on her bed. Maximilian approached her and said: 'I want to invite Ania to a film tomorrow.'

Hans looked at Maximilian, then at Ania.

'You're too late,' he claimed. 'I've already invited her to the cinema tomorrow myself.'

Ania smiled at both of them, saying with a yawn: 'Tomorrow's still a long way off. Don't fight about it.'

I sat down on my bed in a foul mood.

'Go to sleep, all of you; I'm dead tired.'

When I awoke in the morning, the room was dark. Ania's bed was empty, neatly made, as if she had not slept on it that night. It still early. I looked around the room; Hans was also absent, his bed sloppily arranged. Seeing that I was awake, Maximilian jumped from his bed, and a string of curses erupted from his mouth: 'That filthy dog! Crazy son-of-a-bitch!!'

I jumped to my feet, too, and struggling into my clothes, asked: 'What is it? What's happened?'

Maximilian could not restrain himself.

'That bastard! Thinks he's saving our lives, and therefore he imagines he can do whatever he pleases! He...he...made a pass at Ania last night; on my life, I swear he did.'

A cold sweat broke over me.

'How do you know?'

'How do I know – I heard! I saw! He forced his way into her bed. She struggled with him. I guess she was afraid to cry out. So was I, damn it; it's so disgusting, a disgrace – a grown-up man like him...'

I fought to control myself.

'Where's Ania?'

'I don't know.'

What could I do? My hands itched to seize Hans, to break every bone in his body. But I knew I would not do that; I would not even say a word. *We're all in his hands. He's like our landlords, keeping us only as a favour. Our lives are completely dependent on him. He makes his way around the city in an SS uniform, living well enough, and throws us the crumbs of what is left over. But there's a limit to how much we have to pay for those paltry scraps he leaves us.*

Even as I sat brooding, enraged, Ania came into the room,

in her hand a large cup of sour cream.

'I found it at the market,' she said, placing the mug on top of the basket. 'It's really good on bread.'

As she sliced the bread, I saw her hands were trembling.

Maximilian left the room, leaving us by ourselves. We sat down on the basket, chewing the bread dipped in sour cream. If not for the depression in the air, we surely would have enjoyed the heavenly taste of the meal. But the fresh sour cream couldn't relieve the tension between us. The silence grew heavy, unbearable. I looked at Ania, and saw that a crimson flush was spreading over her pale face. The veins in her delicate neck seemed to swell up, and in the deep quiet of the room, I could almost hear her heart, pounding like a hammer.

'Ania, he didn't...?'

Ania glanced at me, her eyes filled with anguish, and she opened her mouth to speak, but could not.

'Don't worry, Annushia, from now on you'll be able to sleep without fear. I'll watch over you at night.'

She finally found her voice.

'I'm just a burden on you,' she said with quiet sorrow. 'Nothing but a burden...'

'Don't talk nonsense,' I said sternly. 'We share this fate, and we'll bear it together.'

'I can't any more...I want so much just to go back home.'

Tears welled up in her eyes. I, too, had to take out my handkerchief to dry my glasses and my damp eyes.

'Come on, little sister,' I told her, 'let's go and find ourselves another place to stay.'

In order to clear the air of the sadness and confusion, I started to hum a song, but it too touched a sensitive chord, a song sung by many youths during those days, youths wandering without a home:

> That tiny white house,
> Engraved in my memory,
> That tiny white house,

Forever in my dreams.
On the window, the sunshine
Sparkles a little,
As if in some eye
Stood a lone tear,
One lone tear, one lone tear...

The song echoed within us both.

The next few days were devoted to finding somewhere to live. Our demands were very few, and we were prepared to take immediately every flat we visited as our new residence. But the task was much more difficult than we had calculated. As in the case of work positions, each landlord requested an official reference from the local authorities. People were extremely cautious. We tried in desperation to act freely, naturally, to bargain with those who wanted to rent apartments, but we did not dare go back to any of them. At each place, we thanked them politely and promised to consider their offers, then went away without intending to return. One woman asked if we were brother and sister.

'No,' we replied, 'but we're distant relatives.'

This woman had a nice, motherly look about her, and I risked asking her if she would agree to leave the apartment registered in her own name during the time we would live there.

The woman's eyes widened in surprise, and then suspicion transformed her features; her face became strange and grave.

'I won't get involved in any shady business,' she declared. 'You had better look for another place.'

'It won't work,' said Ania, when we were back out on the street. 'We're not going to accomplish anything this way; if only we could get help from Kazik or from...Hans Miller.'

She blushed at this last sentence. I made no response; everything inside me rebelled at the thought of turning to Hans. In my mind, I could already hear how he would answer us, how he would grin cynically and say: 'So, in the end, you do come to me... despite everything, eh? When you need me, I'm OK, right?'

Kazik, only Kazik was left; the last resort.

One afternoon, as we returned from our daily search for apartments, two men suddenly approached us, as if they had sprung up out of the earth.

'Papers!!'

I felt the blood drain out of my face, leaving it ashen. Ania also went instantly pale. The two stand very close to us, suffocating us with their presence, and repeat more forcefully: 'Your papers!'

They were in ordinary civilian clothes, and no-one among the passers-by paid any attention to them, or to our distress.

With a supreme effort, I mastered my fear and said: 'We have papers, but what authority do you have to check them?'

In unison, they turned over the lapels of their coats, revealing a round pin with a swastika on it, and one of them told me: 'Don't try to be clever. We're from the Gestapo.' He indicated the pin with his hand. 'We're detectives.'

He showed me his identification; I had trouble reading what was written on it. I was paralysed with terror, thinking only of how to get out of this situation. *If we make a break for it, they'll know in a second that our papers are not all right, and there's no chance we'll succeed in getting away. On the other hand, if we show them our identity cards, there's a chance they'll let us go, but also the possibility that they'll discern that the cards are forged.*

My reflections lasted maybe a minute, no more than that. I had calmed down a little by then, and decided; I reached into the pocket of my coat. One of the men touched the collar of Ania's coat, and his eyes passed over my collar as well.

'There used to be fur here, eh...?'*

I took out my identity card, and Ania did the same. The

---

*   Among the restrictions on the Jews was one requiring them to remove the fur
       from their coats and hand it over to the Germans.

cards resembled one another, despite the difference of the names; they were both new, clean, not folded or wrinkled. I realized in a flash that their cleanness was a terrible flaw, the most blatant of all. The two looked our cards over, checking closely all the stamps.

'Very well done...no denying that...' they stated.

I tried to protest, demanding that they return our papers and leave us alone.

'In a moment we'll leave you, all right – at the Gestapo!' they sneered.

'By what right?' I argued. 'How dare you? Why, our papers are in order!'

'In order?' one of them replied maliciously. 'We'll see about that soon...but just one minute, boy, so you won't say that just anyone is taken to the Gestapo. Are you Jewish or not?'

'No,' I answered. 'But you can see that for yourselves on my identity card. Now, give it back to me!'

'You'll get it back, you'll get it back...over there, at the office of the Gestapo.'

The man especially enjoyed dwelling on the word 'Gestapo', sensing that it sent chills through our bodies.

'Now, move! We'll soon see if you're Jewish or not!'

They pushed us towards the dark hallway in front of the gate of the house we had been standing near.

The first man ordered his assistant to guard Ania in the courtyard. Then, he directed me to the back apartment, opening it with the key he had in his hand.

It was all organized. He turned on a light in the flat, and ordered me to pull down my trousers. There was no way to refuse, and his humiliating check was soon over.

In the courtyard stood the frightened Ania, with the stony-faced creature watching her.

'Here, your friend has come back,' he told her, seeing us emerge. 'Well, how did it go?'

'To the Gestapo!' the officer replied. 'Let's go!'

We entered the street again, now dark. They shoved us

along, two steps ahead of them.

'Let's run for it,' I whispered to Ania. 'You go in one direction, I'll take another.'

'It will never work,' she whispered back. 'And they still have our identity cards.'

What are those cards worth if they can't protect us? I thought. None the less, I was reminded of all the money Father had spent buying them, and of the hopes for us which he placed in them.

'Give us back our papers!' I tried again.

'Only when we reach the Gestapo headquarters. We're almost there.'

'The ring!' hissed Ania. 'Give them the ring. Just so they'll let us go.'

If I had been alone, I thought, I would have tried to escape. I would have broken quickly away, entering courtyards, jumping fences, changing directions, finally hiding, and perhaps then ... but what about Ania? She could never manage all that. I'd be saved, and she'd go to the Gestapo.

So I made the attempt.

'We have a genuine diamond,' I said. 'Give us back our identity cards, and I'll give it to you.'

The two answered without hesitation: 'Show us the diamond first.'

With trembling hands, I took Mother's ring out of a seam in my coat. Even in the darkness, the precious stone flashed with a royal, impressive lightning.

The eyes of our enemies lit up at the sight of the ring. *Mother,* I said to myself silently, *you'll forgive us, I'm sure, for giving your beautiful ring to these scum in exchange for the lives of your children ...*

'Give us back our papers and you can have it,' I said, in a hoarse voice.

The two exchanged glances. It was clear they were not going to give up the diamond. Their decision was whether to let us go, for they could very well demand the ring from us without giving back the identity cards. Possibly they would even get a special reward from the Gestapo for the fine work they had done in preserving the purity of the master race against the pollution of inferior creatures like us.

The awful moments, suspended between life and death, lengthened. The ring was still in my shaking hand, our documents in theirs. Ania was seized by a fit of trembling in her terror. Her chin began to quiver, and her teeth chattered.

Was there a spark of humanity left in these beasts? Maybe they remembered their Christian Jesus, who preached of mercy; perhaps they simply decided to keep for themselves the valuable prize, rather than give it up to the Gestapo. Whatever the reason, I read in their looks that they had made up their minds to settle for the ring, at least for now. For an instant, our documents were grasped in two hands, his and mine; the ring was passed from my hand to his exactly as he relaxed his grip on our identity cards.

Once again, they were ours. I grabbed Ania's hand as she stood, not comprehending what had happened, and we raced away through the streets. Houses, trees flashed by us, and the wind whistled in our ears. After running insanely for several minutes, Ania halted, gasping for breath.

'I can't run any more – I'm exhausted.'

'At least we have warmed up a little,' I tried to joke with her. 'I thought for a few minutes there that you were turning to ice, you were shivering so much.'

The sense of terror would not leave us. Now that those two knew who we were, they could track us to the flat. Such people are not to be trusted. I decided that we both should return to the apartment by different routes. I instructed Ania to choose a long, complicated path, to make it as difficult as possible to be followed.

When we got back to the room, Maximilian and Hans were already there. Hans saw in our eyes that something had happened. He asked, and I related the story. He was stricken with panic, and began to shout: 'You fools! Why did you come back here? Do you want to endanger us as well? Now we're all in trouble!'

We stood, shocked by this reception. This was the last straw. *Just who does he think he is, anyway? Besides, he knows very well that we have nowhere else to go.*

Maximilan was also infected by Hans's fear.

'He's right. Now it's as simple as can be; they'll find your tracks, come to the apartment, and catch all of us at the same time.'

Hans and Maximilian, muttering and cursing, decided to leave the flat and sleep elsewhere that evening. We resolved to stay, no matter what. So we slept, through a long, undisturbed night. The deep and refreshing sleep renewed, to a certain extent, our sagging spirits and strength.

At daybreak, Hans and Maximilian returned. They had wandered all night, each in a different quarter of the city, and never shut their eyes. Seeing us fresh and rested, they relaxed a little; apparently we had not been followed, and the apartment had not been discovered.

A few days passed without any change in our routine. We did a little selling from what was in our basket, and went each day to Stanowski's for mail, but to our dismay, there were no letters for us.

If only I could have spoken with Father, even for just a few minutes, simply to talk, to consult with him. I wanted so badly to hear his opinion about our situation, about Kazik and Wanda and what had happened to Ania at Katya's flat, about Hans and the apartment, work and registration at the Work Office . . . Perhaps Father would be able to tell me what to do. I also wanted to apologize about losing the ring. Father would surely understand; I knew very well that the ring had been basely wrenched out of our possession, but I still felt bad about it. The two men had evidently not been Gestapo detectives at all, merely pretending to be. Many were doing the same thing, and their success fired the imaginations of others. In the intellectual wasteland that had developed, an underworld arose and flowered in sewers and dark basements. My father had never told me that such animals existed. He always emphasized the good and the beautiful, setting them before us as the epitome of mankind, the examples to be followed.

Had it been a lie when we were assured that 'Good always triumphs over evil in the end, justice is always victorious'? Is it really so? I wanted so much to discuss all these questions with Father; maybe then I could have imposed some order on the chaos of my thoughts. But where was he? Who knows what was happening to them at this stage? Those who knew said that the afflictions of anyone trapped in the Ghetto had only just begun.

To my distress, those gloomy predictions were soon borne out, here in Lvov: I was crossing the street one day when I saw a trolley bus, with three cars, filled to bursting with people of our unfortunate race. On the steps of the cars were stationed the armed guards of the SS, their weapons pointed at this herd of humanity stuffed inside: men, women, and children. Another trolley followed, and still another, all of them filled with the same miserable cargo. A fourth and a fifth passed rapidly by, not stopping at any stations, never leaving the centre track.

God, I thought, *do You see how Your people look, your Chosen People? You chose them, but for what? For suffering? For cages? For humiliation?*

The trolleys pass, and nothing happens. Most of those walking to and fro ignore the situation, trying not to look at the frightening convoy. Once in a while, someone is stricken with nausea, and vomits.

I, too, am sick, my guts twisting inside me. I am torn between the desire to survive, to save my life, and the urge to join them, to jump onto one of the cars, to comfort those wretched people by telling them: 'You see, I've come to you, for my place is here, together with you.'

The thought passes; I know there's no sense in it, no use. I returned to the room. Ania came back about half an hour later.

'Did you see?' she asks, stunned.

I nod my head in dumb reply.

At dusk, Hans arrived, accompanied by a woman and child. He tells us that this is Hanna, his sister, and her son. He had taken them off one of the transports. That night, Hans slept on Ania's bed, and Ania had to sleep on his bed, with Hanna and the little boy. I saw how Ania curled up in one corner of the bed, trying to stay away from the strange woman. The three-year-old boy looked as if he was in shock, or maybe Hans had given him a tranquillizer, so he would not cry. His mother held him close in her arms, as if she wanted to return him to her womb, for maybe then she would be better able to defend him.

I asked Hans if there was something else we could do, perhaps, to help others. Hans shrugged his shoulders.

'Even assuming that we manage to remove a few people from the transport, which in itself is nearly impossible,' he said, 'there is nowhere to take those people; there's nowhere to hide. They, too,' he indicated his sister and nephew, 'they can't stay here. I don't know what to do with them.'

That night was horrible for all of us. The woman tossed wildly from side to side, scratching until she drew blood. At midnight, Ania rolled off the bed, curling up on the floor. I covered her with my blanket, and wrapped myself up inside my coat. The night seemed to last an eternity; we waited fearfully for sunrise.

At dawn, Hans dressed meticulously in his SS uniform. In the morning light I saw that the woman's face and hands were covered with small red blotches, and she scratched unceasingly all over her body. The child was still stunned. Ania also began to scratch, especially on the palms of her hands; the rash had not waited long to appear, and she was soon itching all over. The little boy began to cry.

Hans called us together and said: 'Yesterday, more than a thousand people were sent to their deaths; they were shot in the sand, near Yanowska camp. First, the victims were forced to dig a huge hole, and after they had been shot, their bodies were thrown into it. In the meantime, those left in the Ghetto

1 The author's father, taken
in the Ghetto, 1941

2 The author's mother,
taken in the Ghetto, 1941

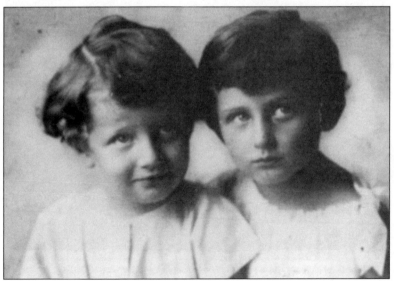

3 The author's elder brother and sister before the war

4 The author sitting between her sister and brother:
represented in the book as 'Reli', 'Ania' and 'Yurek'

5 Miriam and Hanan, 1948

6 Miriam with her daughters, Ronit and Ofri, at Kinereth,
Galilee, 1962

7/8 Miriam and Hanan with their grandchildren

remain. Hanna and the boy must be sent back there. It's for the good of all of us; they're endangering us, and they have no papers. If they're caught here, we'll all be destroyed with them. Someone has to come with us; I'll go first, to check the area, and he'll go along with Hanna and the boy. I'll tell him what to do.'

As he finished speaking, the room was silent. Only the child made a sound, whimpering softly in his mother's arms.

'I'll go,' I said.

Ania jumped up from where she was sitting, her mouth opened, but her voice would not come. I waited; perhaps Maximilian would say: 'You stay behind. I'll go.' But he did not say a word.

Hans had no sentiment at all.

'Hurry, then. Let's go,' he ordered. 'While the city is still quiet. You leave two minutes after me. Let Hanna go a few paces ahead of you.'

We quickly planned our route. Hanna wrapped the boy up, then she covered herself with a large, plaid shawl, carrying him inside it like a peasant woman. I followed her outside, not even saying goodbye to Ania.

For about half an hour I walked, as if bewitched, behind the strange woman. The closer we drew to the area of the Ghetto, I knew, the greater the danger. I could have easily turned in my tracks and disappeared. I could have explained later to Hans... found some excuse. Again and again, I thought about this option, but each time I rejected it, feeling contempt for myself. I had not been raised to avoid responsibility, or to betray someone's trust in me. I had told Hans I would go. So I followed the pair with the feeling that someone else was moving my feet.

Several times along the way, we saw Hans. He looked sure of himself, as if he knew what he was doing. But just as we were approaching the Ghetto, Hans vanished before our very eyes. I was seized with agitation. *Where is Hans? Why doesn't he appear? Why doesn't he give us a sign, tell us where to go? After all, he had said that he would tell us what to do.*

   We were close to the walls of the Ghetto. Hanna stopped and waited for me. For a moment, she handed me the boy, to rest her aching arms. The next instant, a car with four uniformed men, rubber truncheons in their belts, stopped near us. Everything happened in a blur. My eyes went dark, and I felt as if I were falling with the boy into a black, bottomless chasm; as I fell, I flailed and tumbled in the darkness, the empty space...

Chapter Five

After a two-minute ride, they told us to get out of the car. Between Hanna and me was another person, a stranger. At any rate, Hanna was not next to me and she made no attempt to take the boy from me. At the place we had been left was a group of policemen dressed in khaki who surrounded all those who, apparently, had been caught trying to avoid the transport. I realized that we were near the gate to the Ghetto. More than anything else, I wanted to rid myself of the child in my arms. But he was completely petrified with fear, and held on to me with all his might. I would not have believed that a three-year-old child could cling so tightly.

WHERE IS HANNA?? Where is his mother? Let her take him from me; I've got to get free of this child. I must think of myself! After all, she's his mother...

'Hanna! Hanna!' I tried to shout, but my voice could not be heard above the tumult of crying and wails, and the shouts of the policemen who shoved us inside the Ghetto. For a second, I spotted Hanna; her face bore an expression of genuine madness. Her upper body was inclined towards us, while her legs carried her in another direction, along with those being pushed by the rifle-butts and truncheons.

I wanted to move towards her, but she disappeared before my very eyes, and the path to her was blocked. Either on purpose or by chance, two groups were formed: people who were trying, like Hanna, to be saved by proving their age and their ability to do any sort of work, while in the second group, including me, were the children, the elderly and the sick. The people around me were stunned almost senseless, first one old man, then another woman fainting.

Between the two groups there was a gigantic German soldier, nearly seven feet tall, who was riding a huge horse which doubled his terrifying size; he looked like a monster from another world. The little boy's fingers literally cut into my flesh. I did not dare to look into his eyes. Someone pushed by me and cried out: 'Throw that child away! Go over to the other side!'

WHAT DOES HE MEAN, 'throw that child away' – how can you throw a child away?

I tried to explain: 'I'm not even from this city…I was just here by chance…' The man who had given me the advice was no longer even near me.

From the other side, a woman broke away and came over to our group.

'Moisheleh, my Moisheleh, where are you?' A pale, black-haired boy clung to her, and she spoke to him in a broken voice.

'He said', she indicated the German giant, 'that no harm will come to the children, that they'll put them into an institution, an orphanage; they'll take good care of them, so we can leave them. But I just…no…'

Where is Hanna? WHERE IS SHE?? Didn't she hear what the giant had said? Why doesn't she come over? Let her do like that other woman, and she'll be in the same institution with her child…

A woman, very quiet, with a face as grey as parched earth and bloodless lips, but with wise, compassionate eyes, not wild like the eyes of the rest, took the child from me, silently, almost gently.

'There are other children here,' she said, 'three of them mine. I'll take this one, too. I'm staying with them, anyway. In a little while, they're taking us to eat.'

I stood, my feet rooted to the spot. Every spot on my body where the child's fingers had held burned, like an open wound flowing with blood.

One of the Germans had evidently seen what was happening and tried to force me over to the second group – those allowed to live.

'I'm not even from here...I'm not from the Ghetto!' The words I had rehearsed so often spilled from my mouth.

There's nothing to lose, I thought, *you must at least try.*

'He doesn't belong here!' shouted the German.

Polish policemen grabbed me and pulled me outside the gate.

'He doesn't belong here!' They passed the information to a German officer standing outside. A blow struck my cheek.

'If you're not from here, then what the hell are you looking for?'

I tried to take a deep breath, to return the hearing to my ear, the sight to my eye after the vicious blow.

'Papers!' they bellowed.

I took out my identity card.

The Germans don't notice that it is forged. *Just so long as they don't show it to the Poles or Ukrainians*...Someone whispers something into the ear of the German officer, then takes hold of me.

'To Lunskiego!' he roared. 'They'll deal with you there!'

Under the guard of three armed men, I was transferred to the jail.

Before the war, the building on Lunskiego Street was a government office complex. The offices had been turned into prison cells for criminal offenders, and in the course of time, political and Jewish prisoners joined them.

As I arrived at the prison, the sun of the last days of November was rising, November 1942. I looked at the world as God had created it, the earth below and the heavens above, and I breathed deeply the fresh morning air into my lungs, feeling the light breeze on my face. From the moment my feet entered the building, I was robbed of this world.

The prison officials took my papers from me, my head was shaved, and I was thrown into a cell. It was a fairly large

room, which undoubtedly once served as an office for three
or four clerks with their desks. Now, the room was a teeming
mass of ragged creatures, tightly pressed against one another.
At the opening of the door, they all stood up, about sixty in
number. The German policeman shoved me inside, and the
two doors – one regular, and one barred – were efficiently
locked behind me.

Most of the prisoners were weak and enfeebled, curling up
on the floor again, each where he had been standing.

Before I had a chance to understand what was happening,
some of the inmates began to give me 'the treatment'. Using
language filthier than any I had ever heard, they stripped off
all my clothes. Someone tossed me a woollen rag, the shape
of which showed that it had once been a sweater.

'Here, wear this, boy. The lice in it will make sure you
don't feel lonely or special here.'

From one side, someone crawled and stretched out his
hand. 'Come over here, there's room near me,' he said.

'Oh, my God!' I cried out.

'You're calling His name for nothing...' my new
neighbour told me. 'No God has access to this place. The only
visitors here are Satan and his deputies.'

I sat silently, and after a pause, the other boy continued:
'What God do you believe in?'

'The God of Israel!' I replied fiercely, almost without
thinking that by doing so I could be foiling all my desperate
attempts to be identified as an Aryan, to hide my nationality.

'Me, too,' said my new friend. '*Shalom aleichem,*' he blessed
me in Hebrew. We shook hands, embraced, again shook hands.
We smiled at one another, the tears welling up in our eyes.

My new acquaintance was from Lvov, nearly my age, and
his name was Benjamin – 'Beno' for short. He had been put in
the prison about two weeks before me; he already could not
remember exactly when. Beno had been caught on the streets
without the white armband and blue Star of David that
separated the Jews from the rest of humanity. The authorities,
the forces of law and order, viewed this offence as equal to

murder or rape. So Beno was thrown, without a trial, into the midst of the Polish and Ukrainian criminals and killers.

He explained that nobody ever got out of the room we were in; there were no exercise periods, no roll-calls. Every day, a few corpses were dragged out, and several more prisoners taken out and executed without a trial. Each morning, four inmates took out the 'honey bucket', filled with excrement and urine, the only chance for a prisoner to be outside that room of apparitions. As far as Beno could remember, a Jew had never been among those four prisoners; they were always from the strongest criminals in the cell. One hundred grams of bread and one litre of a liquid they called coffee – those were the daily sustenance of an inmate. Soup was given only twice a week.

'Did you notice what sort of floor we're sitting on?' asked Beno. 'It's a parquet floor, well waxed and polished. We're filthy and lice-ridden,' he added, his voice filled with bitter irony, 'and the floor is brilliant. We're forced to polish it daily, with beer bottles.'

'With what?' I asked, uncomprehending.

'Not with beer...' Beno explains, 'with the beer bottles. They put in 20 beer bottles made from thick, green glass, and each day a different group crawls on its knees, pressing and rolling the bottles along the boards.'

'I've never heard of that method before...'

'Everything done in here...well, nobody outside could ever imagine,' Beno replied sadly. 'One boy told me that before I came here, there was a famous Jewish pianist in the cell, Leopold Mintser. He was a very small man, with a hunchback. When he played, no-one ever noticed his deformities; he was a very gifted musician. Here, nobody had heard of him. He was beaten until he died; God was kind to him and took his soul.'

Oh God, help me as well, I said to Him; *I haven't prayed for a long time, haven't asked You for anything. Hear me, as in my childhood, help me, Shemah...Adonai Eloheinu, Adonai echad...*

Beno was speaking to me.

'The only thing that helps me bear it is to remember my childhood...I raise those memories and warm myself inside them.'

Beno's voice seemed very distant, far away. Already I, myself, am far from here, a great distance removed, both in space and time...

Reli, Ania, and I are standing on the balcony of our house on a lovely spring day, a Sunday, free from work or studies. Above us the blue sky, and tiny clouds, white like the foam on the waves of the sea, are sailing across the heavens in the gentle breeze. I am about eight years old, and that morning I had gone with Father to the barber, who gave me a 'young man's' haircut, much to Mother's delight.

On the other side of our balcony, Mother was filling pots with black, fertile earth, and planting pansies in them.

'Oh, how beautiful they are!' cries little Ania, with the big silk ribbon tied like a butterfly in her hair. 'So pretty!' She skips from flower to flower, enchanted by the riot of colours, and by the velvet of the tiny petals of each blossom.

I put my nose into the pretty little flowers, and say in disappointment: 'They don't have any scent...'

Reli, too, smells them, and with the important air of an expert on her wise face, she pronounces:

'That's true. The sweet peas Mother planted last year were both pretty and fragrant. But Mother loves to have a variety, so we'll get to know all the flowers.'

On the balcony next to ours, one floor lower, stands little Teresa, daughter of the Polish physician, Dr Stanowski; with her stood her mother and grey-haired grandmother. Her father, the doctor, who has a limp (he was injured in the First World War), arrives in his car and parks it near the building.

'Father! Father!' cries the little girl.

The doctor locks his car, blowing a kiss to his daughter.

He looks up at our balcony, and we greet him politely with 'Good morning'. He returns our greeting with a smile and is then swallowed up inside the entrance to the building.

'Look, we also have a guest!' says Reli.

'It's Grandfather! Grandfather is coming!' we shout happily.

Our grandfather is a man of impressive appearance, with his blue eyes and long, grey, well-tended beard. Dressed in the traditional black of the pious Jew, he approached us with his measured steps; even his walk aroused respect.

'Mother, Mother!' we cry. 'Grandfather's here!'

'Oh, my goodness . . .' says Mother, putting aside the biscuits she has been baking for the guests coming that evening. 'Heavens, I don't have anything on my hair!'

She runs to the cupboard, pulls out a kerchief and ties it on her head. Grandfather is already ringing the doorbell. We three children run to open the door, Mother behind us.

Grandfather comes inside, his pockets full of delicious sweets. He hugs all of us; it's clear he's pleased with us, and with Mother, too, as she stands with her head modestly covered, as befits his daughter.

On the wall of the hallway hangs a stuffed deer's head, with beautiful, branching antlers. The deer is always silent, his expression never changing. Yet now, somehow, he seems to be smiling around the corners of his eyes . . .

Two days have passed in the jail. They know already that I'm Jewish. There are other Jews here, besides Beno and me, caught with or without papers. Everyone says that they generally collect a large group and execute them all at once, with a single firing squad, in order to avoid the burden of organized operations; they do not wish to devote too much time to such minor matters.

A prisoner who took out the bucket on Tuesday passed me a letter from Ania when he returned. I realized immediately that Hans's hand must have been involved here, that he had managed to get into the prison because of his uniform; that fellow wouldn't even get burnt in a fire.

Dear Yuri,

When Hans came back to the room two days ago, he told me what had happened. It's all his fault. I told him so, and begged him to do something to save you. He said that it looks impossible, for nobody escapes from the place you're in. Still, he promised to try to smuggle in this letter, so I'm rushing to write it, because this may be my goodbye to you. You see – I'm leaving this city. I just can't bear it any longer. I know it's very selfish on my part, that especially now I should stay here, close to you. But I simply can't.

So I'll try to tell you everything briefly. Hans related that you were caught, and that Hanna was sent back to the Ghetto. The boy was taken away with the other children, the elderly, and the weak. They gathered them all together and... and killed them. Hans told me that they had taken you to Lunskiego, a prison for political prisoners.

It seems that his conscience is afflicting him, even this Hans. He treats me very respectfully and gently. I'm just about going mad with the itching from the rash his sister brought. But that's not really important. The main thing is that I'm incapable of being here on my own, without you. I guess I'm not at all brave, despite what everyone thinks. When the real test comes, as now, I'm just a coward.

I went to Stanowski's Pharmacy yesterday; I remembered the address. I asked the pharmacist if I could have any letters for Yurek Kowalik. He stared at me suspiciously, and said that he knew nobody by that name. I continued standing there, like an

idiot, as if my feet were glued to the floor. All of a
sudden, the phone rang. The pharmacist's wife,
who was also there, went to answer it. 'It's from
Cracow,' she said. Instinctively, I took a step
forward. The pharmacist looked at me, then at his
wife holding the receiver. In a mute exchange of
glances, it was agreed that I would take the call.

It's almost unbelievable, such a coincidence;
precisely when I reach the pharmacy, Father calls,
God only knows from where. I was totally flustered.
Everything inside me was crying: Father! Oh,
Father! But I wasn't sure if I was permitted to even
say that word. So I stuttered:

'It's me, I'm here ...'

Father asked me:

'Where's Yurek?'

I didn't know how to answer him, so I just
remained silent. Then I said:

'He's not here ... not with me ... not with me ...'

Father began to press me.

'What happened? Did something go wrong?'

I could tell that Father was trying not to shout.
After a short pause, he said:

'Come back here immediately; otherwise, we'll
lose both of you. Check here for mail two days from
now. I'll write to you and tell you where to come in
Cracow. Then you'll be with us.'

'All right,' I said.

Father was crying as the line went dead. As I
replaced the receiver, the pharmacist handed me
two letters for you, without saying a word. I read
them in bed back at the room, and wept; they were
no longer relevant. Maximilian also told me I should
return home.

'There's the same chance of dying, whether here
or there,' he said, 'and the chance of surviving is slim
no matter where you are.'

To tell the truth, I'm not at all sure I even want to
live any more. I'm wounded, deeply wounded,
Yurek, in spite of the fact that my wounds aren't
visible. But what am I doing – I never meant to start
feeling sorry for myself. Again, I'm being selfish.
Someone should stay near you. I tried to argue with
Maximilian, tell him that I must remain here, to try
to help.

'You won't be able to accomplish a thing,
anyway,' he said. 'If you even approach that area
where he is, they'll catch you as well. If only you
had a kilogram of gold, like Kolnik.'

Some man by the name of Kolnik was released
from Lunskiego prison in exchange for a kilo of
gold. Maybe we'll manage to get some, too. Father
will dig it up, somehow. I'm leaving; please don't be
angry with me, Yurek. Maybe a miracle will occur,
perhaps God will help us; we haven't sinned that
much against Him.

I hope you'll forgive my being a coward. I know
you can't trust in God very much, but I feel so
powerless. I don't know what's waiting for me, or
even if I'll succeed in returning to the Ghetto. Word
has it that from the Ghetto the only path is to the
concentration camps, to the torture camps, where
there are gas chambers and ovens, where they make
soap from . . . human flesh. I don't really believe I'll
survive. But if I remain alive, Yurek, my dearest
brother, you'll be with me, inside me. I don't think
I'll ever have children of my own. Yet if I do, if Reli
and I survive the atrocities, you'll continue to live in
us, you'll appear in the image of our children.

I've got to stop; Hans is waiting. I'm going back
to Reli and our parents. To whom should I pray,
how can I ask for your return? I hope you aren't
suffering too much. I'm not sure if now I could
relate to anyone what we have gone through in the

last month, but maybe someday I will. You were a good brother to me, a dear brother and a friend close to my heart. Farewell.

Your Ania.

The letter was finished; everything was finished. The last thread connected to all that was precious to me had been cut. *Now I'm alone, amidst the rabid wolves; they'll take me out to be killed, maybe tomorrow, maybe the next day. The end has finally come; I'll never get out of this place.*

Fate, however, proved me wrong.

The day after I received Ania's letter, I was listless, indifferent to all that occurred around me; ironically, it was that very moment that a spark of hope was struck. That morning, a uniformed German entered our cell along with the jailer. We all crawled to our feet to stand at attention. Like an electric shock, the news flowed through the group that the Germans were looking for those fit to work. It was forbidden for us to speak, or even to move; so we stood, in a cruel agony of expectation.

The Germans passed among us, scrutinising us from head to toe as if we were cattle at the market. One boy was ordered to stand to the side. Then another. One of the Germans walked by me, and I heard him say to the jailer, in German: 'I need someone with experience in carpentry.'

'I'm a carpenter,' I blurted out.

The jailer began to curse me, wanting to beat me for my audacity, but the German stopped him, pushing him away from me, and eyed me for a moment.

'Right,' he said. 'You, too. Get moving – march!'

It's a miracle, I thought to myself. But I was suddenly stricken with sorrow that I would have to part with Beno. I considered for an instant that maybe it would be better to stay behind in the cell with Beno than to be outside without him. We had supported one another so well during those horrible days in prison.

But then the German stopped in front of Beno and said: '*Du auch!*' ('You, too!')

Things looked fine, now.

Before going out of the gates of the prison, they painted a yellow stripe on our ragged clothes, from top to bottom. At the gate, all the boys chosen from the cell were gathered, everyone branded like cattle. They separated us into two groups; Beno and I were forced to part, yet now that I knew he was also outside the jail, the separation was less painful.

Ten to a group, we were given brief instructions. We were told that we were labour units, that we would work in Yanowska camp and live in the Ghetto.

'If you work hard, you'll get food – soup, every day. But take care that you don't disrupt the order or discipline! You're here to work!'

That same day, they marched us into the camp. Two Germans from the *Wache* (Guards) were in charge of us. As I passed through the streets of Lvov, dressed in rags, marked in yellow with my head shaved like a criminal, several thoughts rushed through my mind. What would happen if Kazik or Wanda saw me? Would they recognize me in my changed clothes, in my present miserable condition? Maybe they would recognize me, and just ignore me? And then again, perhaps they wouldn't – perhaps they would arouse all the city, or at least the underground fighters, to stop the procession and exclaim: 'No! We won't turn you over to them! We'll defend you!'

I was seized by a desire that they should see me, if only to put them to the test. But neither Kazik nor Wanda was visible anywhere. No one tried to stop the march. Nobody tried to fight for us.

We arrived at the camp: a large area, very large, fenced all around at a great height with rolls of barbed wire on the upper edges. At the gate to the camp stood a guard shack, and in front of it many soldiers and snarling dogs. We received an order to halt. The guards accompanying us passed some documents to the sentries, explaining something to them.

'Enter one by one!' resounded the order.

The sentry began to count.

'*Eins, zwei, drei, ... neun, zehn.*'

When the first one had finished, another sentry also counted us.

'*Eins, zwei, drei, vier, funf...*'

After him, a third guard counted. Finally, the sentries stamped the papers our guards had brought, and then ordered us to enter the camp. Unlike the residents of the camp, who were never allowed to leave, we were designated to return to the Ghetto each evening, hence the careful counting.

The camp was silent, desolate; vacant fields and long barracks. In one spot, I saw a group of prisoners, like us with shaven heads and clothes with the yellow stripe, hard at their labour. A group of Nazi soldiers, no fewer in number than the workers, was goading them, pressing them to work faster lest they should neglect their labour even long enough to straighten their backs for a moment. The trained dogs paced around the soldiers, ready to rip a worker to shreds at a sign from their masters.

We reached the building site. Awaiting us there were professional builders who passed out tools. Our task was to erect observation posts along the barbed-wire fences of the camp. We were told that we must complete the work in exactly the time allotted for it.

'We're warning you,' said the contractors, 'this is no game. Out there, in the sand,' they indicated a vast area outside the fence, 'out there they shoot masses, hundreds of thousands, all in one grave. The clothes they gather up into bundles, and trucks filled with clothing are sent to the *Lumpenwascherei* [the rag laundry].'

We worked without a break until nightfall. After work, we received bread and sausage; because we had begun work late that day, we were not given soup. There were no handouts here, just hard labour.

Leaving the camp at dusk, we were again counted three times at the guards' shack near the gate; ten is a nice, round number. It was about an hour's walk back to the Ghetto. My legs were wobbly with fatigue and weakness. How long could I stand up under this sort of work? Who had it better, those already destroyed or those whose strength and energy were sucked out before they were killed?

Near the gate to the Ghetto, once again the triple guard; more stamping of papers and counting, as if we were a shipment of cargo. Inside the Ghetto, we are left on our own, after being told to be at the gate at dawn. The boys from Lvov have somewhere to go, at least. I and three others are homeless. We have been given an address, but are dismayed when reaching the apartment to find there were already eighteen people in the room, so our reception was less than warm, to say the least. After all, our addition robbed the present tenants of a little more of the air they breathed in the stifling room. Dejected and sore, I laid myself down under a table without undressing, merely taking off my shoes.

I remember what Beno had said: 'Only the memories of my childhood help me to bear it...'

> *It's a large playroom, filled with light. The walls are painted a pale blue, the furniture is ivory-coloured. On the window is a curtain which is a work of art: flowers sewn with silk thread are strewn over its surface. On the wall hangs a picture of a beautiful young woman, surely a princess. She wears a spring dress, and her head bears a crown made of a single large narcissus blossom. This picture is not a painting at all, but rather needlework, and not done in threads but in tiny beads the size of the head of a pin.*
>
> *I am nine, and I'm perched on top of the cupboard. Why had I climbed up there, anyway? I was cross with everyone ... Reli was practising constantly on the piano, for the date of her recital at the Conservatory was drawing near. Almost every day, Karol came to visit her; that priggish little boy, always dressed like such a dandy in his pressed suit with the gold buttons, as if he were going to a dinner party. They sit and play fourhanded; the Mozart sonata is truly beautiful, but they play it endlessly and I'm sick of hearing it.*

Ania does whatever comes into her head. She grabs my things, and when I take them back she starts screaming; then I'm told: 'Let her have it; after all, she's just a little girl ...' For me – nothing. I'm just supposed to do my lessons for school, and also my chores at home, that's all.

So I climbed up on top of the cupboard to jump. True, I hadn't thought it was so tall ... Reli and Ania stand below and tease me:

'You won't jump, you're afraid ... you'll never jump ...'

'I will, I will jump!' I declare in a brazen decision.

'No, you won't, you're scared – you won't jump ...' continue to taunt me.

'I WILL jump!' I cry, and then I DO jump, just to show them, just so everyone will know that when I say something I mean it.

But, ouch, what's wrong with my leg? It really hurts.

Reli and Ania help me to my feet.

'It's nothing,' I grin, but nevertheless, I'm not able to stand up.

Mother is at my side in a second. For a moment, I'm afraid of her reaction; maybe she'll be angry with me and say: 'What a child – what's wrong with you?!' But she looks at me with loving eyes and says: 'You're very brave, a real hero!'

They put me to bed and call the doctor. Father comes home early from work. I lie in bed, wearing new pyjamas. Orders are given to prepare all my favourite foods. Mother sits next to me, telling me stories, showing me pictures in the photo album. Then she sings for me; when Mother sings, anyone who hears is lost in another world. She sings about a fairy princess who lives in a crystal palace on a glass mountain. Mother also likes a more serious song, about a young peasant girl named Manka, who leaves the boy who loves her to follow a rich lord. Finally, when I'm warm and drowsy, she sings the lullaby we all love best:

Shining star, in the sky, my baby wants to sleep.
Fold your hands, close your eyes, my stories will
make you dream.
Once there was a famous king, who had a lovely
daughter;
They lived in a garden, full of lilies, and never knew
sorrow.
But suddenly there struck a cruel and terrible fate:
A dog came and ate the king, the princess became a
mouse.
Don't cry now, my little one, for I've a secret for you:
The king was made of chocolate, the princess of
pink creme.

*I am sleepy, calm. Let the dog have his delicious meal, let
him enjoy the chocolate king, and even the
mouse... There are no worries, no danger, everything is
fine.*

  *Mother tucks me in, so gently... I'm so content, so
warm...*

Someone is shaking me, roughly.
  'Get up, quick! It's already daylight! We're leaving for
work.'
  I crawl out from under the table, tying my shoes on in a
hurry. My legs ache; the muscles are still tight from the
punishing labour of the previous day. I rush to the
collection point. Everyone is already there; again, they
count us, once, twice, three times. There are ten of us. As
before, we march to Yanowska. I try not to let them see how
difficult it is for me to walk. Despite my efforts, they seem
to notice.
  'Get moving, there! Go on!' shouts the guard; this time,
only one guard accompanies us.
  At the gate of the camp, we are again counted. In the
evening, we go back to the Ghetto after another day of cruel
labour, barely able to drag our feet. As we draw near the

Ghetto, the guard suddenly sees that one prisoner is missing. He counts again:

'Eins, zwei, drei, ... acht, neun.' The tenth is absent.

'That's it!' he shouts angrily. 'They'll hang you all!! From the balconies of the houses in the Ghetto they'll hang you, as an example for all to see!'

We continue on our way. The German searches his pockets, pulling out a piece of candy. When he sees there is no-one nearby, he gives it to me: 'To sweeten the last hours,' he says.

After a moment, he adds: 'I'm not the one who started all this...'

We arrive at the Ghetto. 'Our' German pulls out the papers. He speaks with those at the gate, explaining something to them. All of a sudden, I feel a light push, and to my astonishment, I notice that we are no longer even nine, but only four. I break away, running with great strides, no longer feeling the pain in my legs at all, and I'm soon swallowed up in the close, dense darkness of the Ghetto streets. Behind me I hear shots, cries of 'Halt!' – yet I don't stop. I pass alongside the houses, hidden in their shadows. At one spot, an open gate beckoned; I enter it, and slump down in a black, foul-smelling hallway. The shooting ceased. Total silence. I had no idea how the others had fared.

Where should I go? Which door should I knock on? Whom should I ask for shelter? Who would give me different clothes, without that damning yellow stripe?

I remembered the first Jews who arrived in Cracow, refugees from Germany; the community had given them food and clothing. I decided to go to the offices of the Lvov Jewish congregation. I got to my feet, and then someone descended the steps. I asked him: 'Where are the congregation's offices here?' and he informed me that they were very close by, three buildings away.

Cautiously, fearfully, I move into the street and reach the other building. Not a soul is in the entrance; only its stench and desertion greet me. The tension grips me like a vice. In the hallway are doors leading into different rooms. Some distance away, I discern a small figure. A minute later, a boy of about twelve is standing before me, striking a match. I see a pale face, eyes sunk deep into their sockets.

'What do you want here?' he whispered.

'This is the congregation's offices,' I replied, 'they were at work here during the day.'

He surveys me in my prison garb.

'Don't expect anything from those working here. They're all bought.'

For an instant, there was silence.

'Are you hungry?' asks the youth.

But there's one thought which is occupying me more than that of food.

'Listen,' I tell him, 'you must, you absolutely must do something for me.'

'What?'

'Get me something to write with, paper and an envelope. I've got to write immediately to my parents, and you must see to it that the letter is sent.'

What a nerve, I thought abruptly; what right do I have to give this boy such tasks? Don't I know that it's been a long time since any mail has left the different Ghettos? Why, it's impossible even to have light here – even the utilities office is empty.

To my surprise, the young boy returned a few minutes later with a pot of soup and some slices of bread, as well as paper, pen, and an envelope. He even brought a candle and matches.

'When you've finished writing, give the letter to me. You can depend on me – I'll see that the letter is sent. In a second I'll bring you something to cover up with, so you'll be able to sleep here.'

This boy is an angel, my heart tells me so; after the war I'll make sure that they give him a medal for heroism. After the war? Oh, when will that be...will there ever be a time after the war? What will tomorrow bring? Indeed, what does await us tomorrow??

The soup the boy had brought went down with difficulty.

I saved the candle for the writing of the letter; *if I write quickly, perhaps I'll be able to finish* . . .

> My dearest parents and sisters,
>   I'm writing 'sisters', for I assume that Ania is already back with you. Hard as the situation is where you all are, I'm glad Ania decided to return.
>   As for me, I'm in the Lvov Ghetto, in the Jewish congregation's office. A boy who was here gave me this paper, a pen, and an envelope . . .

Continuing the letter, I related all that had happened to me since I was caught, five days ago. I wrote about Lunskiego prison, where I had been sure the end was near. I told them of Beno and the others, how the German came to pick young men for work. I described how I had declared myself a carpenter, how that had saved my life. I wrote about the ten in our work group, and about escape after the guard's words when he found one of us missing. I also told them how we fled when we realized we had nothing left to lose, succeeding in ducking away under a shower of gunfire.

> . . . yet it's not so easy to escape, with a shaved head and no other clothes, without money or someone to help.
>   Tomorrow morning, I'm going to try to do something. Maybe I'll succeed in locating Beno; I don't know how, though. I'm very easy prey for those looking for opportunities to prove their loyalty and efficiency to the Germans. I want to live, so very much; there are so many things I want to do which I haven't begun yet. If I survive, someday soon I'll have to examine my conscience. We, as a nation, will have to settle accounts one of these days with some of the other nations, and with ourselves as well. Why did all this happen to us? Where is the God we believed in? Does He

help only the strong? Only those who know how
to help themselves? It seems to me that this is the
true state of affairs, and if we survive, we must
remember it. We must not allow the coming
generations to experience what we have, not ever.

The candle is growing shorter. After it has
gone out, all I will have is the cold, black night,
and I'll spend it on the table where I am writing
to you, now.

If I live, I'll give you some sort of sign. If not, I
will share the fate of the boys not long ago, who
were seen by all the Ghetto, their young bodies
swaying at the ends of ropes, above the balconies of
the flats.

I realize how painful it must be for you to read
this letter. But then, you wouldn't want me to
disappear without first telling you that I can see you
all here, around me, your precious faces that I love
so well are close to me...I'll see you after the candle
goes out, even in the total darkness, with the coming
of the final destruction. You surround me, like a
protective wall; you'll be with me until the last
moment. I feel warm in the love you've always
given me.

The candle is flickering...Mother, come, come
closer, yet closer...I want to feel your gentle hands,
your calming touch. Father, Mother, cover me up,
I'm so cold...Search for me, Father, everywhere.
Perhaps we'll meet there, in the next world. Reli,
Ania, please don't forget...

Darkness has fallen, blackness, and I didn't
quite...

The night continued, and another day never broke.

ANIA

Chapter Six

The dark autumn of 1942 was cold and lonely. Nobody was waiting for Ania at the Cracow railway station. *It is another Cracow,* she thought leaving the train. *The one I loved, the one from before the war, has left us. True, my family is still here, but they are all within the walls of the Ghetto. Nobody should know that. It is a great secret. But then, nobody really cares. People have their own worries. When one of us is beyond the walls nobody can know that he or she is a Jew. For all the Jews, just as anyone who helps them, are condemned to death.*

When she was leaving the station a boy, a few years older than she was, called after her: 'Hey you, wait!' She panicked and walked faster. *To be out of his sight as soon as possible.* She knew the situation from Lvov. *Is it possible he has recognized me?* She lost him when she turned into the street off the main road.

She remembered the address of the factory where Father and Reli worked – Deutsche Küstenfabrik – and that was where she went. She knew they would always leave the Ghetto at dawn and return to it every evening at dusk. A month before she had walked out with them, clinging to Father's back, hidden under his loose coat. Afterwards she left them, took her armband off and disappeared into the Polish crowd. Now she would have to do everything in reverse order. Returning to the Ghetto is not easy either. You are counted at the gates three times and each time the number must be the same.

Father waited for her at the gates of the factory. She was struck by the way he looked: the hunched figure, sunken cheeks, and his eyes so infinitely sad. Not so long ago before he had still been tall and lean with sparks of joy in his eyes. *How can one change so much?*

She heard Father sob, although he did not cry. He was calm but she could hear him weep. He took her to a modest-looking flat. A frightened woman let them in and locked the door behind them. She gave Ania a plate of soup and a slice of bread. Ania realized Father had arranged that treat earlier. The woman must have helped him from time to time. He sat opposite Ania watching, with sad and hungry eyes, the soup and bread disappear from the plate.

Later, Father told her to join one of the groups returning to the Ghetto. Reli was also in that group. She had lost weight during the previous month. Her legs were covered with ulcers and when marching in her column she tried to hide her limp. At the gates the people entering were being counted. Her group had come back with one person too many, but Ania somehow sneaked in. Nobody paid any attention to her.

Mum and Grandma were already at home. Ania ran into her mother's arms. 'Mummy,' she whispered.

Mum stroked her hair and tears ran down her cheeks.

'I couldn't have *not* come back,' Ania explained. 'I couldn't have been alone...'

'How long were you alone...since...since he had left?'

'Since when he had gone with that child.'

'What child?'

She looked at her parents helplessly. They did not know anything.

'I don't know what happened myself,' she whispered. 'Izio just didn't come back.'

'I have a feeling he is still alive,' Mum said; and Father asked: 'Where is the ring I gave you to buy yourselves out?'

'They took it from us,' Ania said quietly and shuddered at the memory of that nightmare. The crooks who caught them in a quiet Lvov street and told Izio to strip so that he could prove he was a Jew, and then tricked them out of the ring.

They lapsed into silence. After a while Father asked: 'And

how about the basket? And all those things which were in it?'

'I left them. I left everything with the people we lived with,' Ania said slowly, overwhelmed by terrible guilt. 'Those people, they will give everything back to us after the war,' she added, but without much conviction, her eyes focused on the floor.

'Let her be, Hesiek,' Mum said. 'If only Izio were alive there would be nothing to regret. Come Ania,' she added in a lighter voice, 'come, we will go and see the children. They will be so happy to see you.'

It was only then she found out that after she had left for Lvov the children had been taken to the orphanage. Nobody had time to take care of them when she was not there. The same day Mum and Ania brought the children back home. Araleh, Aaron and Ella were very pale, their heads were infested with lice and Aaron had earache. The children clung to Ania as if she were their natural mother. She was only 15.

She got down to work at once. The children were neglected and hungry for love. Ania's taking care of them meant salvation not only for them but also for her. It justified her return from the Aryan side, her giving up on the fight for life.

A few days later, when everybody except for Grandma the children and Ania were at work, Ania saw a white envelope on the doorstep. There was no mail service in the Ghetto, which meant someone had come to bring the letter specially. She reached for the envelope, picked it up, opened...and a spasmodic cry escaped her lips. From Izio! Still holding the letter in her hand she collapsed onto the nearest bed, unable to control herself, crying hysterically and in convulsions. Hearing those unusual noises – alternate cries and sobs – the children came running out of the kitchen and surrounded the bed. Little Aaron brought her a glass of water and Ella lay down next to her. Seven-year-old Araleh, the oldest one, could already read and he understood what was going on. The spasms, which Ania could not control, lasted a good few minutes. Then suddenly she pushed Ella away: 'Don't come near me! You can't! I'll infect you with scabies, just the way I caught it myself... in Lvov...' Ania was scratching herself until she bled and little Ella walked away. She only shrugged her shoulders as if trying to say she could not care less – if Ania were in pain she could be in pain too. Then all four of them began to laugh and shout with joy: 'Izio's alive! Izio's alive! He has written!'

Ania could not wait to see her parents; she dressed the children and they all went outside. 'We shall wait for Father and Reli and show them the letter from Izio immediately after they have walked through the gates!'

The street was crowded and it stank, although orderly cleaners (one of whom was a friend of Ania and Izio – Mieciu, Mieciu-Smieciu, Mieciu-the-Rubbish-Man as they called him for a laugh, without spite; he was alone – his parents, both of them pharmacists, 'had gone' during the October *Aktion* to Belzec)* were cleaning the Ghetto and getting rid of the garbage and dead bodies. But there was too much rubbish and too many corpses for them to handle and they could not manage. That is why the Ghetto was so dirty, and it stank. Hungry children in tatters stood at the street corner selling something; or were they just begging? Ania did not pay attention to anything. At that moment nothing was more important than the white envelope with the letter from Izio.

Here is Küstenfabrik. There go the people, hungry and tired, after ten hours of slaving at work. They walk through the gates in fives, counted by the guards – German, Polish, Jewish. Here is Father walking through the gates, hunched, sunken, frighteningly sad.

'Daddy!' she shouted to him. 'Daddy, our Izio is alive! Look!'

Father straightened up at once; his eyes shot towards Izio's

---

* Belzec was an extermination camp in the region of Zamosc operating from 1 November to 30 June 1943, and was mainly for the Jews deported from the Ghettos of Cracow, Lublin and Radom. The people who were brought to Belzec were then killed in gas chambers with car fumes. The number of victims of Belzec amounts to 600,000 people.

letter and sparkled. For a split second he reminded her of the Father from before the war. They got Reli out of her line of five and they laughed and cried while hugging one another. Aaron, Araleh and Ella, who watched them from afar, were laughing and crying as well. They elbowed their way through the throng of people returning from work. At some point they were joined by Mum, who was on her way back from Madritsch.* When they got home they read Izio's letter ten, twenty times, and while reading they sank deeper and deeper into helplessness and despair.

'What are we to do? What to do?' Father looked at Mother and Mother looked at Father, and then everybody looked at Ania.

'What?! Am I to go back to Lvov? Do you want me to go back to Lvov?' Her heart froze. They did not answer and Ania grappled with her thoughts and told them – or maybe she told herself – that nobody knew where to look for him. *How can you find one boy in a foreign city, in this awful muddle, amidst the black surging billows of destruction swallowing hundreds of thousands of victims each day? How to find our poor Izio?* She did not stir and they all helplessly kept silent. Ella sat in Ania's lap; Aaron cuddled up to her, nestling against her left-hand and Araleh against her right-hand-side. The children behaved as if letting her know she could not go. They could not be left alone for the third time.

'Scabies,' Ania reminded them, freeing herself. Ella reluctantly climbed off her lap. Ania cooked the children something to eat and put them to bed. Her parents did not get a wink of sleep that night.

The next day arrived and a new worry with it. The police came, *Jüdische Ordnungsdienst*, and they arrested Reli. Somebody must have informed on them. The police had searched the attic and found Ania's Aryan *Kennkarte*. Mum

---

* Julius Madritsch was a German, a 'Righteous Among the Nations' (the medal awarded by Yad Vashem in Jerusalem to the non-Jews who during the Nazi occupation risked their lives to save Jews).

pushed Ania into the wardrobe; it was very dark inside. *No night is as dark as the inside of the wardrobe*, Ania thought, short of breath, and scratching herself until she bled. Mum stood in front of the wardrobe, pale as a sheet. One of the OD-men put the *Kennkarte* with Ania's photo under her nose and yelled wildly: 'Where is this girl? Where is the owner of this *Kennkarte*?'

The second OD-man was already searching under the beds and the third one, with a cynical smile on his face, walked into the room holding frightened Reli by her collar. Reli had just returned from Pankiewicz's Pharmacy* with the ointment for scabies they had ordered a few days before. 'Here she is!' he exclaimed triumphantly. 'Here is the criminal! Arrest her!'

The poor desperate parents were caught between the devil and the deep blue sea: to deny it, to say it was not her, would mean a further search and then the police would most certainly find Ania, 'the real criminal'. On the other hand, to let them arrest innocent Reli...

'It is not her,' mumbled Mum with her white lips, and the fourth OD-man came closer and said, almost friendly: 'If you can prove it we might let you buy her out.'

'Bastards, scum, swine!' Never before had they heard Father use words like that. He was one of those people who weighed their words carefully, as he was very sensitive about the rules he referred to as *Kinderstube*. 'Bastards, scum!' He was unable to control himself any longer. The police had already left the flat forcibly, taking Reli with them, although she had managed to drop the jar of the precious grey ointment bought at Pankiewicz's on the floor.

Ania, bleeding from the scratches, came out of the wardrobe.

---

* Tadeusz Pankiewicz was a Polish pharmacist, the owner of a pharmacy in the Ghetto, where he lived himself, sharing the fate of its inhabitants and ▒em any way he could. In 1947 he published his memoirs in Cracow. ▒called *The Pharmacy in the Cracow Ghetto*, was translated into Hebrew. ▒varded the 'Righteous Among the Nations' medal.

'We must hide her,' said Mum. 'They cannot find her. They will kill her.'

They wrapped Ania in shawls and led her out of the flat to the Borsteins', who agreed to give her shelter for a few days, putting their own lives at risk – on the condition that she would not infect them with scabies. 'That', they said, 'could be worse than death itself.'

'Don't worry,' Mum said. 'The disease isn't contagious any more, now that we have this ointment.'

Then there was the struggle to save Reli. The parents looked for someone who would back their case up. They sought connections with influential people – the ones who had befriended the authorities, in other words the scum, the mean people who had no scruples about hurting their brothers in misery. People like that would ruin their friends just to ingratiate themselves with those in power, to help them get rich and become rich themselves along the way. Reli was kept in the Little OD Prison, in the Ghetto. It was not as bad as the Montelupich Prison,* but here the prisoners were also tortured and interrogated; here they were also killed... Most of the female prisoners caught on the Aryan side pleaded innocent, claiming they were not Jewish at all. But there were many informers. And they would say: 'I used to know this lady before the war. Of course, she is Jewish.' And so the next morning she was hanged or shot, unless she was lucky and somebody bought her out of jail for a lot of money. In Reli's case at the very beginning, an important mediator was bribed. He let the family know it was possible to prove Reli's innocence as well as the fact that the *Kennkarte* did not belong to her. That is, if the authorities were well paid for all the pains they would have to take in the process.

---

* The Montelupich Prison was a prison in Cracow. During the war it was the Gestapo prison where many thousands of political prisoners and members of the Resistance, both Polish and Jewish, were kept in custody. Most prisoners, having been interrogated and tortured, were then deported to concentration camps but the prison was also the site of mass executions.

Father was completely ruined. There was no more news from Izio. He had been swallowed up by the bottomless pit of destruction. Reli came back home sad and changed by all the death she had seen. After buying her out of jail there was no more money for another bribe. That meant we were absolutely defenceless. Father contemplated suicide again. 'To leave the gas on in the kitchen or to get some potassium cyanide,' he said, 'is better than what is ahead of us.' Father, a faithful believer in the God of Israel, always praying to Him, was choosing death. Mum was doing everything she could, begging him to abandon the thought for our sake and the sake of the other three children.

But then it was not only Father who wanted to put an end to his life and was looking for dignified liberation in death. Ania thought about it as well. The scabies was not bothering her that much now that she had the ointment, but since that time in Lvov she had not had her period and she got it into her head that she was pregnant. She did not have much sexual experience, nor did she know much about sex for that matter. She knew something from Irka and the books about love. There had been no talk of love, of course, but Ania intuitively knew that Hans had tried to rape her and she feared the worst. Her parents were so broken that there was no way she could have talked with them about something like that. It would have been like rubbing salt into their open wounds. And so, ashamed and miserable, not knowing how to deal with the situation, she decided to kill herself. She had already thought a few times about how to make use of the axe she chopped the wood with. Not such a long time before, already in the Ghetto, she had read *Crime and Punishment* by Dostoyevski. If Raskolnikov could kill that woman with an axe, then Ania could kill herself. It could not be such a grave sin, so she was not afraid of the punishment. On the contrary, she felt she had already been severely punished; God only knew for what crime. *But*, Ania thought with dread, *what if death does not come? I could strike a blow, wound myself and end up handicapped for life. I will be even more of a burden for my parents...No!* The vision of a failed attempt discouraged her from suicide.

In Plaszow, just south of Cracow, they were building a concentration camp, called KL Plaszow. People talked about the nearing closure of the Ghetto. 'All the people able to work will be transported to Plaszow, where they will live and work; and those who do not work...They will be able to work in Plaszow as well. There is enough work since most of the Germans have been mobilized. They need to be replaced, they need to be provided with everything they want, to make them happy, satiated, so they could let others live...' That was what people were saying. And that was what they wanted to believe. 'Even children will find work in Plaszow...'

Father did not believe it that much. He and Reli were still going out to work at Küstenfabrik, but they did not feel safe there. Many people wanted to work for Emalienwarenfabrik of Oskar Schindler,* a businessman, since the Jews who worked for him felt safe. But there was not work for everyone there. Mum worked for the Madritsch tailor's company. Madritsch, who (together with his free labour force) was mass manufacturing uniforms for German soldiers, provided his slaves with better working conditions. He gave them better soup and even let them take some food home for their families. Mum would always bring home some soup for Grandma, for Ania and for the children, because ever since she had come back from Lvov, Ania had stopped sneaking out of the Ghetto in search of something to eat. 'Our employers will save us,' people were saying in the Ghetto, and they wanted to believe it. But then the young boys and the young girls from the underground killed that hope. They distributed leaflets on

---

* Oskar Schindler ran an enamelware factory in occupied Cracow and employed Jews. He saved the lives of 'his' 1,200 Jews (Steven Spielberg's film *Schindler's List* was based on his story).

behalf on *The Fighting Chalutz*.* In their newsletter, Dolek Liebeskind, the leader of the Jewish Combat Organization in Cracow, and Szymszon Dränger, the editor of *The Fighting Chalutz*** wrote:

'WE DO NOT BELIEVE THEM'

'We,' wrote Dolek Liebeskind, 'shall fight not for our lives but for having our four lines in History.'

'Those are sublime words,' said Mum, 'but I do not know how to fight for History. We fight for every minute of our lives – we want to survive.'

A few days later the Ghetto had various contradictory bits of news of the attack by the Jewish Combat Organization and People's Army on the 'Cyganeria' café, which was swarming with the Gestapo and SS-men. People were frightened, they knew that the Ghetto would be severely punished, but most of them felt some relief, even though this was but a drop of justice in the sea of ghastly atrocities. Dolek Liebeskind, Szymszon Dränger, his beloved Gusta-Justyna† and others paid for it with their lives.

The Ghetto was engulfed in sorrow and hopelessness, and the lies and slander which were deliberately being spread confused and disorientated even the most sensible people. At night the Jewish authorities working for the Germans would call at houses with long lists of names. They would get people out of their beds, they would not allow them to take anything

---

* He'chalutz ha'lochem (Hebrew) – literally 'The Fighting Pioneer' – was the name of the newsletter issued by ZOB in the Cracow Ghetto. Its main editor was Szymszon Dränger, one of the heroes of the Cracow Ghetto.
** ZOB (Zydowska Organizacja Bojowa) – the Jewish Combat Organization – was a defence organization created under the leadership of Mordecai Anielewicz.
† 'Justyna' was the code name for Gusta Davidsohn-Dränger, the wife of Szymszon (Szymek) Dränger. When held in the Montelupich Prison she kept a ̶ ̶ ̶ ̶ ̶slips of toilet paper. After the war her diary was published under the *Diary of Justyna* (translated into Hebrew). Szymek and Gusta, who ̶ ̶red at the same time – in November 1943 – are heroes of the Cracow

or to say goodbye to anyone, and then they would take them away. Nobody knew who had made this 'black list,' but people knew that those who were taken away would disappear for ever. People would go into hiding wherever they could but the possibilities were becoming fewer and fewer. Nobody provided an explanation; on the contrary. When going out to work outside of the Ghetto people would pack all the necessary things into their knapsacks, as they did not know whether they were going to return or not.

On 13 March 1943, people stood in their groups as usual, waiting to go out to work. Every day Dad and Reli walked out to work, but they did not know whether after they were done the guards would take them to the camp in Plaszow instead of bringing them back to the Ghetto.

On that same day Mum did not even get to Optima Square, where Madritsch had his tailor's company. Together with all his workers, still in their groups of five, she ended up in Plaszow that very morning. People were marching out of the Ghetto in fives – the tension was higher than usual – and suddenly panic struck. They understood that those 'able to work' were leaving and the 'unable' were to remain in the Ghetto, forced into 'Ghetto B' with its orphanage and hospital. Amon Goeth* – a fat, ponderous giant with a whip in his hand and a gun at his belt – came riding on horseback through the streets. He was accompanied by two huge fierce dogs, which were barking wildly. At the gates of the Ghetto, scrupulous OD-men were counting the people marching out: 5, 10, 15, 20, 25…They were hastening them with their crops. You could hear them yell: *'Los! Los! Raus!'*

As Ania was dressing the children, and combing their hair, she could hear people running up and down the stairs and she could hear the shouts: *'Zur Arbeit, los schnell, raus!'* She realized that something horrible was going on and she was on her own

---

* SS-Untersturmführer Amon Goeth was the Commandant of the Plaszow camp from February 1943 to autumn 1944, and was renowned for his exceptional cruelty. After the war he was sentenced in Poland as a war criminal and sentenced to death by the Supreme National Tribunal.

with the children. She shuddered and her blood froze in her veins. She went out of the flat and nervously knocked on their neighbours' door. There was nobody in. Not any more. She ran one floor up – the doors were open, the flats empty, things scattered on the floor. The same downstairs. There was nobody in the entire three-storey building but herself and the children. It made her blood run cold and she could feel her legs turn to jelly. The children were waiting for her in the open door of their flat; all of them were quiet and pale. On the streets they were already shooting and Aaron's left ear was hurting him even more. With trembling hands Ania gathered together a few jumpers, some shawls. She told the children to hold hands and walked out with them into the street. The street was crowded with 'fives'; nobody cared about their workplaces any more. The OD-men were marching the young and healthy out of the Ghetto. The pavements were swarming with fainting mothers and their children: OD-men were separating them by force. The mothers were screaming, crying: 'Kill me – but I'm not leaving here without my child.' The women were being beaten and kicked and their children were being thrown around like rubbish.

Then the OD-men changed their method. 'All the children must be taken to the orphanage,' they ordered. 'It is for their own good,' they were saying. 'The orphanage is already full of children,' they were saying. 'They are being taken care of by guardians, by good people,' they were saying. 'Tomorrow the entire orphanage will be transported to Plaszow and there the children will be working for the Germans as well. Yes, children also can be useful. Goeth himself said that – go and ask him if you don't believe us.'

Mothers were at their wits' end, trying to get anywhere near the giant on the horse. At that very moment Goeth took out his gun and started shooting at the people from the back of his horse. The crowd stood back; those killed were removed. OD-men were snatching the children out of their mothers' arms and forcing them into the 'fives'. Some mothers were nervously pushing their babies into their knapsacks, but at the gates the knapsacks were being pierced with bayonets...Ania was petrified, the children were huddling together, surrounding her like chicks. They were being pushed at from all sides. In one of the leaving 'fives' she spotted Grandma! She had lost sight of Grandma in the morning, and then, suddenly, Ania saw her, her cheeks flushed, marching like a young woman. Nobody pushed her out of the line – she got out. She saved herself.

'And so shall we,' Ania said, dragging the children behind her and mingling with the marching 'fives'.

'Are you crazy, girl? The children won't make it, you won't manage to do it...'

They were thrown out of the line – once, twice, three times – and the shooting was becoming more frenzied, there were more yells and more dogs barking.

'My ear hurts,' said little Aaron when, finally thrown out of the marching 'fives', they found themselves among 'the unable'.

Ania leaned over him: 'Soon,' she said, not knowing herself what she meant by that.

'Soon?' asked Ella, ''cause I am so tired!'

'Soon,' repeated Ania. *That bastard Goeth. Let him come and shoot us.*

The streets were less crowded now. Most of the people had left the Ghetto already. The rest were herded into 'Ghetto B.' That was where they gathered the sick, the elderly, the children, and all those whom the butchers did not like.

Rela Perlman, the elder daughter of Aunt Mania, walked past them with two of her children. *And where was her eldest, ten-year-old Beni?*

'Beni went with his father. He managed to get out, he pretended to be an adult,' said Rela, reading the question in Ania's eyes. 'With these ones,' she pointed to her two younger children, 'I will go to the orphanage.'

'We will go together.' Ania wanted to join in, to die or to be with an adult, to share her responsibility with someone.

Rela said: 'What are you doing here? Why are you not trying to save yourself?'

At that very moment somebody gave her a push and in an instant the children were on one side and she was on the other. It was a lawyer, Dr Wasserlauf, a friend of Father, and he had come out of nowhere. *Had Father asked him to save Ania? If he were unable to save all the children then to save her at least?* Ania never asked Father about it and she never saw Doctor Wasserlauf after that day. At that moment he was standing between her and the children and she was already being pushed at from all sides, the crowd was already being rushed at with the whips and crops; the OD-men were shooting again. A woman was shot; she fell down beside her. Somebody pulled Ania into a 'five'; the group was marching towards the gates, out of the Ghetto. Ania tried to establish eye contact with the children she had left behind but they were not looking at her anymore.

Rela Perlman was walking towards 'Ghetto B' followed by a group of children.

Chapter Seven

The sun set. The large ball was descending from the sky in its usual manner. Just like every other day. As if nothing had happened.

Under the leaden sky gigantic barracks had grown on the grounds of the old Jewish Cemetery in Plaszow. Frightened, exhausted people, driven through the streets of Cracow as if they were a herd of cattle, were reaching the hill of Plaszow. Dad, Mum and Reli waited on the hill until Ania came, together with the last fives. They hugged her and kissed her, holding back the tears, asking no questions. Only other people were saying that '...but of course! The children would come, those who had stayed in the Ghetto, all the Jewish children from Cracow would come the next day.'

More yells and more rushing. Women and men went to their barracks separately. Mum, Reli, Ania and several hundred other women were herded into theirs. It looked just like a huge, long, narrow warehouse; along the walls and in the middle stood three-tier wooden bunk beds, reminding Ania of shelves in the shop. On top of them went 'the merchandise', placed with maximum space-efficiency: body next to body.

Ania lay between her mother and sister. Here – with her left-hand side touching her mother's body and her right-hand side stuck to her sister's – was her 'home' now. Mum and Reli, who had been there since the morning, told her the latrine was over there...

Why had I not stayed with the children in the Ghetto? Ania was killing herself with guilt, feeling physical pain in her heart, as if it were being cut with a blunt knife. Through the bleeding heart she heard Reli's quiet voice:

'Here, on the bottom berth, just below us, is our grandma. She made it by a miracle.' Reli said.

'I know,' Ania answered.

The next morning, at dawn, more yells. The roll-call! *'Alle raus!'* Everybody – all the camp, men and women, to the *Appellplatz*. The news travelled like electric current through the rows of people: 'The children! They are bringing the children!' The whole camp froze in anticipation. The degenerate 'Chlopczyca',* an androgynous monster in an officer's uniform, with a crop in her hand, was counting the rows.

Suddenly, a few goods delivery trucks drove through the square and went towards Hujowa Górka.** At the same time people were being hanged at the *Appellplatz*. 'Chlopczyca' was forcing everybody to look at the scaffolds and at the bodies of the hanged people swaying in the wind. Ania, her heart almost not beating, was listening to the echo coming from the side of the 'death hill', seeing in her mind's eye little Ella, Araleh and Aaron. *There they are, standing there in a group, hugging one another – and looking at her with their bright eyes.*

Her daydreaming was brutally interrupted by a harsh command: *'Feuer!'* Instinctively she turned away from the sight. In that very instant 'Chlopczyca' ran up to her and slapped Ania with all her might. Ania hardly managed to stand still. Her head was spinning, she could feel her teeth shaking in their sockets.

'Schauen!' 'Chlopczyca' was yelling straight into her ear.

---

* 'Chlopczyca' was a well-known member of the Plaszow female camp crew, blindly following all the orders of Commandant Goeth and often surpassing her superiors in tormenting the prisoners. [The nickname, here used as a proper noun, could be approximated by the English adjective 'Butch', and it is used to describe a woman who looks, behaves or dresses as a man.]

** Hujowa Górka was a hill on the territory of the Plaszow camp, the site of individual and mass executions. The name derives from SS-Oberscharführer Albert Hujor, who carried out the shooting there. [The name in Polish carries a double meaning, 'chujowa' (although spelt differently the pronunciation is the same) being a vulgarism and in the above context meaning 'fucked'.]

Ania was looking ahead, at the scaffolds, but she could no longer see anything. In vain did she try to recall the previous vision – the bright eyes of little Ella, Aaron and Araleh were never to return. The children – together with the other Cracow children – had disappeared for ever.

Petrified with fear and dread, people stood on the *Appellplatz*. The execution continued.

For one year and seven months we lived in KL Plaszow. How many days? How many hours?

Mum, Reli and Ania, and with them seven other women, would sit, for ten hours each day, at one of the huge tables in *Stickerei* and, under the supervision of an OD-man, Kapo Wasserstrum, make stockings and jumpers for the Germans. There were maybe twenty tables like that in *Strickerei*; each with ten female workers.

A part of the barrack was screened with a curtain. This was where Wasserstrum, his wife and their son lived. The smells of fried omelettes, tomato salads and other delicacies wafted from behind the curtain, irritating the starving bowels of the working women.

They would get a portion of soup from the cauldron once a day. Wasserstrum would give out the soup himself. One by one they would come and get one ladle of the liquid, which did not smell too good. A half an hour break for queueing, eating, going to the toilet (more queueing), and already Wasserstrum was rushing them back to work. It was then that the smells of fried omelettes would begin to spread from behind the curtain. Ania often thought that she should stand up and open that curtain: if everybody saw the three of them sitting there at the proper table, eating, they would attack them and kill them. But nothing of that sort happened. Ania did not move, out of weakness, out of fear. If somebody else did, she would join in...Perhaps...But nobody budged and Wasserstrum after his dinner would return to work with greater enthusiasm, slapping his handyman – a lawyer, Dr

Licht – for not being able to force us to work faster and better.

At Ania's table there was a woman, Mrs X, with her two daughters, Ada and Bela. Her youngest daughter, Cipora, was being hidden by a Polish family. Nobody asked for details – you were not supposed to know. Mrs X would often sigh and wipe the tears from her eyes; sometimes she would smile sadly to herself.

At another table there were two beautiful fair-haired girls – Zosia and Frydzia Edder. Their parents 'had gone' during the October *Aktion* in the Cracow Ghetto. The sisters would stick together desperately. 'Two people are still a family,' Frydzia would say. They did everything not to get separated. Until the typhoid fever and death came and took pretty Zosia away. Frydzia was left all alone.

At her table there was one more 'family' like that: the young, fragile sisters Blitz, from Oswiecim.

'Oswiecim?'

'Yes. Until the war it was an ordinary town. Many Jews, all our family...'

'And now?'

'The town is probably all the same,' Rajzia Blitz thought for a while and said. She was skinny; her eyes were bulging out of hunger, or perhaps as a result of some untreated disease. *She will never make it through the selection,* thought Ania – from the day of the closure of the Ghetto experienced in selections.

Ania had already known by then about the existence of the camp in Oswiecim. In the first months of the war the whole of Cracow had heard of the arrest of the Jagiellonian University professors (many of whom used to live not far from Ania's home in a nice, large building at the corner of Lobzowska and Aleje Slowackiego). At that time the Germans had also arrested other 'dangerous criminals', and then, people learnt, they were all sent to the camp in Sachsenhausen. There was also talk about Oswiecim, and people talked with much dread. This was a prison camp for the people arrested for sabotage and for political prisoners (for instance, communists) who were kept in extremely harsh conditions. 'The guilty' were being sent to Oswiecim without a court sentence, often only on the basis of informants' accusations. Here nobody was particularly impressed. 'What court had sentenced us for the slavery in Plaszow?' Inhuman anarchy was omnipresent and fear stupefied people. The families of the Oswiecim prisoners would sometimes at least receive letters from their loved ones which they could answer. The prisoners could also get medicine and parcels. 'And we here in Plaszow? Plaszow is not better than Oswiecim,' people would say. 'Is Oswiecim like Dachau? Is it better or worse?'

'What is Oswiecim like?' Ania would ask Rajzia. She had heard that after the attack on the 'Cyganeria' café, when Dolek Liebeskind had been shot, his companions were sent to Oswiecim.

Rajzia shrugged her shoulders: 'A town like any other. Until the Germans came, there were many Jews there. The Jewish community was the same as anywhere else – the temples, cheders*...In Oswiecim we used to go to Bet-Yaakov,'** She pointed at her sister and herself.

'And now?'

'I don't think so much has changed. Only there are no Jews. Everything that is not Jewish is still there.'

'And that camp? Where is that camp?'

Rajzia shrugged her shoulders again: 'I don't think I even know. There was no camp before the war.'

'Shh...*zex*,'† Rywcia, Rajzia's sister, warned them. Wasser-

---

* Cheder is a Jewish religious school for boys between three and thirteen years old. Older boys would attend Polish schools and after school they would go to the cheder because parents usually cared about the religious education of their children, especially boys.

** Bet-Yaakov is a Jewish school for girls. Because it was not recognized by the Polish Ministry of Education girls would attend Polish schools and some of them would also go to Bet-Yaakov.

† *zex* was a word taken from the criminal slang and in the camp code was used as a warning.

strum with his killer face and the crop in his hand was walking through the room. The conversations stopped, everybody went silent, hundreds of heads bowed down over the German stockings. Ania, like a squirrel, sneaked under the tables back into her place by her daily supply of stockings and began to sew eagerly, one stitch at a time.

Wasserstrum yelled at the other end of the room; cursed: 'You whores! You do not appreciate my efforts to keep good living conditions in *Stickerei*. Fuck you! You will see, you will learn the way we work here!' And all the time he was waving his crop in the air, hitting the tables, and you could see that he was restraining himself from hitting the women. Ania jumped up, ready to do something, she did not know what herself, but Mum on one side and Reli on the other grabbed her by the hands and forced her to stay put. She shrank down. *After the war she would kill him with her bare hands*, she thought.

After the inspection whispers could be heard again in the room.

On the other side of the room, at the last table, sat the Wanderer sisters. A little bit older: one was 20, the other 21 years old. Both of them had Aryan looks, were tall and handsome, spoke beautiful Polish.

They too? Ania wondered. *If I were their age*, she thought, *and if, just like them, I did not have parents any more and, like them, I did not have any children yet, would I let them take me to this hell?*

But they did let them; they must have had no choice. Their presence was good for other women. The Wanderer sisters could recite beautifully. In between *zexes* they would entertain the women during the sad and boring hours of work, reciting known poems, improvising comedy shows and songs.

At the next table, on the other side, sat the elder Mrs Bornstein with her three adult daughters, one of them already married herself. Her husband, Ania's uncle, had got stuck in Lvov, with the Soviets. The second Bornstein girl, so pretty, intelligent and clever, fought like a lion to better the conditions for her mother and her married sister, to get better soup, a better place on the berth. For them she was ready to give up her own rations. 'They have to survive,' she would say. 'Their husbands are going to wait for them; they have someone to live for.'

Ania's grandmother, zealous and hard-working, obviously believing that obedience and work were going to save her, sat at one table with the religious Aunt Mania and her youngest daughter, 16-year-old Renia. Aunt Mania and Grandma were constantly praying; they trusted in God completely. 'God protects us all,' Aunt Mania would say.

Oh Auntie, why had God not protected your elder daughter Rela and her little children? Why had He not protected Araleh and little Aaron and Ella, who was only five years old? What evil things had they done to Him?

And Auntie would go on: 'This is God's will, and we should thank God, and praise God.'

Doesn't she have eyes? Can't she see what's happening? Shall I tell her how horrible it was during the last day of the Ghetto? How the elderly, the sick and the children were cruelly killed in cold blood? If this is God's will, then what sort of God is He? How can one praise Him?

'Mania has it easier,' Mum would often say, looking at Aunt Mania praying to God.

Mum would secretly sell sweets, one sweet for a slice of bread.

'If someone has as much faith as she, they find it easier to withstand all this.'

Ania kept silent. She could not understand. She was hungry.

'Perhaps you could take a box of sweets and go around the room,' Mum suggested, 'before Wasserstrum gets out from behind the curtain. Go, Ania. Maybe someone will buy one?'

Ania hesitated. Mum was not set on the business either. She would rather wait until somebody came to her with a slice of bread and suggested the exchange for a sweet. Only Aunt Mania would buy one sweet a day and give sometimes one and a half slices of bread for it. Thanking God for everything and asking Him for nothing.

In the morning, they were driven out of their barracks onto the *Appellplatz*. People would hurry for the roll-call, starved and frightened, rushed with yells and lashes. At the *Appellplatz* 'Chlopczyca', and other Germans in uniforms, all of them Amon Goeth's people, were inspecting the rows. The square was often the site of executions and other forms of punishment – 25s, 50s.* Those who were not looking would get the same, or would even be killed. Even when there was no hanging or beating at the *Appellplatz* the Germans would often drag people out of their rows – people whom, for one reason or another, they did not like – and they would send them to 'Hujowa Górka'. Nobody ever came back from there.

After the roll-call people would go to their workplaces. Apart from *Stickerei* there was a tailor's workshop as well as a carpenter's, a paper workshop, and probably many more. Those working in one did not know what was going on in the other. In each of them people were left to a different *Kapo*, *Aufseherin*, *Blockälterster* and themselves. You would stay for at least ten hours a day in the workshops, in truly claustrophobic conditions and isolation. Still it was better than other work in the camp. Men – Daddy among them – after the morning roll-call would leave under an armed escort to return before the night exhausted to their barracks, straight into their berths. Coming back from these escapades Daddy once brought a box of sweets, and sometimes he would bring some bread. The protégés worked in the camp kitchen; some women got work as maids at the houses of the Germans working in Plaszow. There was also a sickroom in Plaszow, that is a small hospital,

---

* 25s, 50s were 25 or 50 lashes with a stick on naked flesh: the punishment used in camps for minor misdemeanour. The graver 'the crime' the more lashes; there could even be 80. *The Eighty-First Lash* is the title of the Israeli documentary, ~ritten and directed by an Israeli poet, Chaim Guri. The title symbolizes the ͐ar inability to understand the concentration camp survivors by the ͐rael. For the film hero, who in the camp was punished with 80 ͐ eighty-first lash.

but they were not curing people there. People were afraid to go to hospital. They knew it was one more implement of extermination. There was also some kind of an office.

And there was 'Hujowa Górka', or 'the death hill', an important workplace, an important post.

The camp was built on the site of the old Jewish Cemetery and, as a form of entertainment, some prisoners would be selected at random to dig up the graveyard. They were told to dig the bodies out of the graves, put them in a heap and set fire to them. The smell of death, hard to stand, was hanging over the entire camp, making people sick, making them dizzy. The Germans were wearing hygienic facemasks. Amon Goeth's and other 'masters" dogs, were set on the barely alive slaves to make them work faster. More than once the fangs of those dogs – all a part of the SS-men's favourite training – bit though the live flesh of the working people. Those who could not stand that were thrown among the corpses taken out of the graves and burnt.

On the 'hill' they were trying out a different scenario: here day after day they would bring trucks full of Jews caught on the Aryan side – mainly women and children. They were told to strip naked; they were shot and burnt.

'Criminals', i.e. those who had tried to escape or to commit sabotage, were hanged at the *Appellplatz*, a few at a time, before the very eyes of the whole camp. When the bodies were still twitching in agony, Amon Goeth, the Camp Commandant, would shoot at the standing people from the balcony of his flat, just for fun. His assistants, in order to ingratiate themselves with their superior, were ready to invent multiple other forms of 'entertainment'.

Without her wig Grandma did not look herself at all. Ania looked at her and tried to remember the pre-war Grandma, elegant, in her impressive blonde wig. Grandma had changed completely. Her eyes did not shine any more, they were filled with fear. Everyone had changed. Only Aunt Mania still had her gentle eyes.

Where does Aunt Mania get all that serenity from? And where does she find all those shawls to wear on her head?

'God will not forsake us,' says Auntie Mania, pouring naphtha out of the bucket straight onto Reni's head, swarming with lice.

What do you mean that 'God will not forsake us'? He has already forsaken us. What else can happen?

'Do not sin, Ania,' says Aunt Mania, even though Ania is not talking to anyone, keeping all her thoughts to herself. The evening comes; hundreds of women in the barrack move about the three-tier bunk beds, their bodies rubbing against one another.

'It could have been much worse,' says her aunt. 'You should be thankful to God for what there is. See? We have some naphtha left in the bucket. It is for you, Ania, for your head.'

'No!' Ania would not have it. 'I don't want that disgusting naphtha! And I am not going to be thankful!'

A moment later, however, she took the bucket and shared the naphtha with Reli and Mum. They all had lice. If you wanted to wash yourself in the cold water you had to queue in the latrine. Naphtha, if you could get it, helped for one day, then the lice would return.

Mum was still trying to save her favourite green angora dress, even though by now it smelled of naphtha and its stitches were swarming with large white lice. Mum had worn that dress the day she had left the house, in that other world, in Cracow, in Lobzowska Street, when they had been given 24 hours to move quickly into the Ghetto. 'It is warm, and it does not crease. I am sure it will come in handy one day,' Mum had said then, packing the most necessary things in a hurry. She could not have known that lice were going to like that very dress more than other dresses made of rough fabrics, which were not as nice to touch. On Mum's leg you could see a huge boil. It was filling up with pus and the leg was as hard as stone. The boil turned into a carbuncle and the carbuncle into a phlegmon. Mum could hardly walk, her leg hurt so much, and there was a threat of blood poisoning. The illness had to be hidden – with a leg like that you could not be *arbeitsfähig* (able to work), and they liked to shoot such people there, on the hill.

Ania sneaked out of her barrack and walked towards the men's barracks on the other side of the camp. She was waiting for Father. As she was walking she could feel a sharp pain in her knee and ankle. *It must have been because of that work in the sewers, when she had been standing in the ice-cold water for a couple of hours.* One day before they had taken her out of *Stickerei* to work in the sewers, God knows for what. She had been freezing there, feeling that something bad was happening to her joints. *But it was better to do anything, she thought, rather than blaspheme and dig the dead out of their graves – for that was the kind of work she could have been forced to do as well.* Five, six yelling Germans had run into the workshop the day before and the helpful Wasserstrum had provided them with a workforce without a word of objection. As many people as they wanted. In exchange for which his wife could make herself a new dress from army wool.

'How can she have no shame?'

'Do you expect people like that feel shame? Well, true – until the war Father and I did protect you from people of that sort,' said Mum. 'Until the war you did not know people like that existed.'

Poor parents, thought Ania, *it must be very difficult for them not to be able to protect us now.* Ania had stopped noticing the pain in her leg. She had to see Father. *Perhaps he would somehow know what to do.*

She hardly recognized him. His clothes, marked with yellow paint from top to bottom, were hanging loose on his skinny body. When he took his cap off, she looked with dread at his deformed, disfigured head, marred by the so-called *Läusenpromenade.** *What are they doing to us, these Germans?*

---

* *Läusenpromenade* – literally 'the promenade for lice'. Male prisoners had a 6–7 cms-wide lane shaven around their heads. It was one more method of humiliating and ridiculing people, as well as making it more difficult for them to plan their escape.

God, God, how can You let it happen? But Daddy prayed to You every day! Where are You now, O Lord?! How about people?

'And you walked through the streets like that?'

Father was silent. You could see he wanted to say something about walking through the streets of the town but he could not. He was so sad that Ania had no courage to tell him about Mum's condition. They stood between the barracks and kept silent.

It was a peaceful hour; the camp inmates were taking advantage of it. Hidden by the twilight, men would sneak out to see women, women to see men. Ania had already known that at that very time in the barracks, on some berths, people were being introduced, getting engaged, getting married. That you could hear whispers, creaks, sighs. She had been told it was done in a hurry, because nobody was sure of the next day and some of them wanted still to know life.

Father and Ania were following with their eyes the frenzied commotion between the men's and women's barracks. Finally Father said: 'I haven't got anything for you today.'

'It doesn't matter, Daddy,' said Ania.

'How's Mum?' he asked.

Ania mumbled something and let her head drop. Father had tears in his eyes, he was saying quietly: 'All my life I believed...thought...planned...Mum wanted us to go to Palestine...I waited. I was well off, I thought we had time. I was wrong. Now it's killing me. Because we could have been...'

They stood in silence for a while longer and then Father took Ania's little hand through the barbed wire. He kissed it. After that he turned back and walked towards the men's barracks with heavy steps. Ania stood as if glued to the ground, bringing her hand to her heart, and saving Father's last kiss for ever on it. She stood there, looking at the beloved silhouette slowly disappearing into the darkness.

A few days later she could not leave her berth; she could not take one step. Her feet and hands had swollen and she had a fever. Mum, concealing her own phlegmon, came up to the *Blockälteste* and said: 'She cannot go to the roll-call today. Only today... I'm sure she'll be well very soon and she'll be back at work. With young people like her fever goes up quickly and it goes down quickly as well.'

'To hospital,' decided the *Blockälteste* and dismissed Ania from the roll-call and her work.

There was no choice. Mum and Ania joined the long queue of sick people, who, knowing the risk – as these queues at the *Krankenstube** were often inspected – had no choice but to go there. After a long wait they were seen by a young doctor, Schindel. Mum racked her brains trying to remember common friends from before the war, mentioning names to get better treatment from the doctor, but he did not pay any attention to her. He examined Ania thoroughly, asked her a few questions, took her blood to be tested.

'Nobody, not a single woman in the camp gets her period,' said Dr Schindel after hearing her answer to the question he had asked. 'It's the Germans taking care of the hygiene in the camp. They must be adding bromine to the soup,' he explained. 'They can invent all sorts of things. Their imagination has no limits.'

'But I, even before the camp...' mumbled Ania, blushing.

The young doctor understood her fear, tried to calm her down, even to make her laugh. Not even Mum could understand the cryptic exchange between the two of them and she looked at Ania in surprise. Then they were told to wait in the hall for the blood test results.

After an hour the doctor said: 'The girl has been living in great stress, she has acute inflammation of the joints and a seriously damaged heart. She must go to hospital.'

Ania was pleased. She felt great relief that she did not have to worry about her condition any more. She felt so bad that in her own mind hospital seemed the most appropriate place to be and she dreamt about being able to lie down. *Oh please, let*

---

* The *Krankenstube* – a sickroom in the camp hospital.

them have a normal bed in this hospital, clean sheets and good care, please! Mum was worried, though.

'I'll do my best to help her,' Dr Schindel reassured her.

So maybe Auntie Mania is right when she says that you have to be thankful to God for everything? Thank You God, even though You truly are cruel, thank You that in those terrible times there are still good people around, and thank You that we have a hospital here...

Only the hospital was not a real hospital. The half-dead patients, rising to their feet, were made to stand at the roll-call every morning here as well. The person leading the *Kommando* which supervised the roll-call was a female officer. She marched like a man in her SS uniform, in a skirt, with her face clean-shaven like those of the men. It was the same 'Chlopczyca' who had slapped Ania's face...then...when they had brought the children. Here also she was slapping the faces of the sick during the roll-call. The wards were relatively clean, although the patients were a mess. Better care was taken of scrubbing the floor than of curing the patients, who were lying in twos or threes on one berth, unwashed and undernourished. You could only dream of a normal bed with clean sheets.

In the evening Ania had a visitor – little Dzidzia, Ania's friend from their short school years and their private classes in the Ghetto, which had also finished so soon. Dzidzia worked in the paper workshop with her sister Stenia and their father who, being a professional, was somehow important there. Ania remembered what Dzidzia had told her about their mum – who 'had gone' in the October *Aktion* – and about their grandma and grandpa who had been shot in front of her very eyes. Out of the five girls who used to have classes together in the Ghetto three had come to cheer Ania up when she had returned from Lvov. Little Ella was no longer there.

Dzidzia was holding a pot of soup in her hands. 'It's for you,' she said. 'It's good soup.'

'Is it your ration?' Ania asked.

'No, I have already eaten mine. I'm not hungry. You eat.'

Ania wanted to thank her and say something nice, but her head was empty. *What did we use to talk about...before the war?* She could not remember.

'Out of our five there are only the two of us left; you and me,' said Dzidzia, standing next to Ania's berth, which she shared with one more sick woman she did not even know.

Ania bit her lip and did not say anything. Dzidzia on the other hand knew more about what was going on in the camp: 'There are still more transports coming to Plaszow,' she told Ania. 'Jewish women and children caught on the Aryan side are shot on the spot. Political prisoners, those brought from the Montelupich, both Poles and Jews, are hanged. Ten OD-men from the Cracow Ghetto, including Chilowicz and his wife,* were murdered and dismembered; the whole camp had to walk pass that massacre and witness their end. Remember them, Ania?'

'Is there anybody from the Cracow Ghetto who would not remember? Their vulgarity, their horrible Polish, their primitiveness and eagerness to carry out their contemptible work!'

'The Germans used them as much as they could and, you see, they got rid of them themselves. It was a terrible sight. So many crushed skulls...'

The other sick woman, Ania's bedmate, got hold of their blanket and pulled it onto her side.

'Don't let go of this part of the blanket,' said Dzidzia in irritation and continued to let Ania in on the news. 'Large transports of Jews from the neighbourhood and from Slovakia are passing through Plaszow on their way to...But why am I telling you all this? The war will be over real soon, you'll see, Ania. Everybody says that.'

'On their way to where?'

---

* Chilowicz Wilhelm and Chilowicz Maria were a couple of degenerate and grotesque OD-people ruling the Cracow Ghetto. They were profoundly hated for ingratiating themselves with the Germans, tormenting the Jews and stealing from them. On 13 August 1944 they were shot by the Germans in Plaszow. Their dead bodies were exhibited and all the prisoners were forced to come and look at them.

Dzidzia was not sure and she did not answer the last question. She took the empty pot and left. Ania was totally exhausted by the fever and the massive dose of medicine she had been given, all aimed at putting her back on her feet really fast. She went out like a light.

A few days later people began to say that the hospital was going to be cleared of the sick. Most of the patients were in a terrible state and depressed. Some were trying to save themselves. Reli, her face transparent and her cheeks sunken, came to help Ania get out. She was clearing a path for her younger sister, who was crawling behind her in pain. 'You must be well,' she was telling Ania, as if it depended on her.

'Nothing depends on us.' Ania repeated the words she had heard before without thinking. 'We are in God's hands.'

'God?' Reli smiled bitterly. 'Aunt Mania was taken away, even though she was such a believer. Her Renia is all alone. Our grandma is gone as well. You should know how brutal they were with them. People like Aunt Mania or Grandma are to save the munitions industry of the Great Reich.'

'Where to?'

'A few hundred women were deported to Skarzysko.* People say it's where they have huge German munitions works and prisoners are worked to death doing the hardest and most dangerous work. They do not get paid and they have no rights. Poor Grandma! She wanted to live so much. She won't manage; she won't make it through.'

Reli and Ania crawled into the barrack. Mum, wearing a bandage soaked in ichthyol ointment, was waiting for them on the berth. Her lips were trembling, she could neither say

---

* Skarzysko-Kamienna was a town with a labour camp attached to the munitions works, 'Hasag', operating between August 1942 and July 1944. The camp was filled with Polish, French, Dutch, German and Hungarian Jews: 8,000 people on the average. The prisoners worked in the munitions works and in the tailor's and shoemaker's workshops at the site of the camp. During an epidemic of typhoid fever approximately 15 people died each day. Many of the prisoners were shot by the Germans. After the closure of the camp those left alive were deported to Czestochowa, Leipzig and Buchenwald.

anything nor stop her tears. The three of them huddled up and cuddled each other

'Your grandma wanted so much to live,' said Mum in a trembling voice. 'When is this going to end?'

'Never,' whispered Ania. 'Because, even if we survive, this hell will never leave us.' Mum and Reli were silent.

Days went by, weeks, months. Cold was getting to them, hunger paralysed the brain, all their thoughts concentrated on food. They were often moved from one place to another, from one barrack to another, and each change was for the worse. In the meantime there was news of the Germans being defeated on the Eastern Front; news that their armies were retreating in panic and the front line was nearing Cracow.

Is it so? Have we survived? Have we lived to see the end of it? Will they let us live to see the end of it?

Alongside that other, much worse news, was reaching the camp. All the camp was like a steaming cauldron full of boiling water having nowhere to go. To the camp were coming transports of Jews from Hungary, driven wildly in great haste like cattle, having been dragged straight from their real houses, on their way through Plaszow to Oswiecim.

What are they going to do with all these people in Oswiecim? Instead of Oswiecim they would say 'Auschwitz' now and they would not mention what was done with people there. You could hear the names of other camps as well: Trzebinia, Buchenwald, Gross-Rosen, Mauthausen, Stutthof. Trains were coming to Plaszow – terrible freight cars, not meant for carrying passengers, which were hastily filled with people who were maltreated and tortured until they could not take any more. Carried off into the unknown, they were leaving their liberation far behind.

On the 'death hill' they were carrying out executions with greater frequency.

How did Daddy know that both younger sisters of his and Aunt Mania, Hania and Hela, together with Hania's 15-year-old

daughter, Irka, were brought, despite their Aryan papers, to the hill – in those last days of Plaszow – and shot? Who had told him that terrible news? Was it the poor, unhappy Olek-Tedy, Hania's husband and Irka's father who lived with Daddy in the same barrack? Was he the one who had found out about that? Or was it some friendly Kapo, *helping out there on the hill, who had told them?* Ania was totally shattered by that news. Aunt Hela was for Izio, for Reli and herself, like a second mother. Ania saw her for the last time when her aunt had sneaked into the Ghetto from the Aryan side, risking her life to bring them the money from the sale of the grand piano (it was before Ania and Izio went to Lvov).

'It's hard to sell anything now,' Aunt Hela had told them then. 'For furniture, lamps, carpets, paintings – they pay nothing...for the grand piano, they showed mercy and paid. They did not have to...' Aunt Hela had given them the money, said goodbye and left.

'Where are you going?' Ania had asked her then.

'We're going from place to place,' Aunt Hela had answered sadly and gone away.

They had been going from place to place and they had come here, up the hill. Hela and the beautiful Hania, Ania's favourite aunt. Hania had had an unquiet soul; she had lived in constant confusion, struggling in her thoughts whether to choose Poland or Palestine, assimilation or emigration, Polishness or Jewishness. Fate had decided.

And, together with them, Irka. The 15-year-old Irka, Ania's cousin and best friend. Her faithful guide through all the things on earth. *How was she to go through life without her advice?* Ania was tormented by the feeling of longing for her loved ones, whom she kept losing for ever, one by one. In the good old days she had thought that Izio and Irka were going to be a couple. She would have liked so much to dance at their wedding! They had been so close to her, they had been her life, they had been her – a part of her. You cannot lose so many loved ones at one time. Your heart cannot take it.

And how about Irka's baby sister, the five-year-old Ninka-Dana?
Did they shoot her as well? Many children were shot on the hill,
even the younger ones – especially the younger ones; all the
children from the May 'children *Aktion'* during which the ten-
year-old Beni Perlman, the one who had managed to get out of
the Ghetto, 'had gone' as well. All those children had been shot
on the hill – but nobody had seen that little girl. *Was it a miracle*
and she had stayed hidden somewhere? Where? For how long? Who
is going to keep her, who is going to collect her one day if there is no-
one left alive? Ania could not think any more. From the days of
her illness her senses were not as sharp as they used to be, her
memory did not keep as much as before, before she was ill.
Only a few scenes remained with her for ever.

Scene one:

A column of men marches through Plaszow. Freight cars
marked 'Buchenwald' are waiting on the tracks. Ania,
mingled into the groups of men standing at the roll-call, is
looking for Father. She finds him at last, runs up to him,
even though they are lashing at her and chasing her away
from all sides. 'It's not my turn,' Daddy is saying. He is
strangely excited. 'You know Ania, at this *Appellplatz*,
amongst hundreds of unknown men who are being herded
into the cars like cattle, I saw my nephew from Chrzanów.
I had not seen him for years. Reli and you did not know
him at all. Meir. Son of my brother, Menasze. Menasze fell
during the first war and Meir grew up without a father. In
spite of that he was the best student in *yeshiva*. I felt guilty.
There we were, living in our beautiful Cracow, in riches,
and they in the *shtetl* were hard up, hardly making ends
meet. And now here...we're all equal...He did not
recognize me, but I recognized him immediately...It's good
I had a piece of bread with me – I gave it to him for the
road...'
    It is hell all around us and Daddy is talking about the
family, about feelings. The trains keep on leaving, their

wheels rumbling on the tracks, screams and lamentations are rising high into the indifferent sky, the leaving people disappear into the thick fog – and darkness.

Scene two:

A similar situation. The men are standing on the *Appellplatz*. On the tracks are freight cars marked 'Mauthausen'. Ania sneaks out and finds Father, who is saying: 'My time has come. We're being deported.'

Ania is cuddling up to Father. Only now does she realize how skinny he has become. Skin and bones. There are macabre scenes to witness. People are being handled into the cars in an inhuman way. Ania would like to hide under Father's coat again, like on that day when she came back to the Ghetto. She would like to go with him, even into that freight car. But this time Father has no coat and she is being chased away. These terrifying cars – and this Mauthausen – are meant for men only.

Father – like an ill man who appears better a moment before dying – looks well now. He leans over Ania and whispers into her ear: 'I'm leaving now. You go back to Mum and Reli. You're still together...Stay together...and watch over one another. And especially...you take care of Mum...if I can't do it...do it for me...'

Those were his last words.

Then something awful happens. Father disappears, the train leaves, people disappear, the square becomes empty, Ania can hardly stand, surrounded by screams and yells and her ears full of Father's last words: 'Take care of Mummy, do it for me.' It is dark.

Scene three:

In Plaszow the women are returning from work to their barracks. They are marching in long columns, in fives, their legs heavy like lead, feet dragging. Mum, Reli and Ania are marching together in one group of five. On the bend the silhouette of a man comes out of the shadow and approaches them with a dish in his hand. Ania's senses are blunt – she cannot see, cannot hear, cannot feel. But that silhouette gets a reaction out of her. *Daddy?* Her heart is pounding, tearing out of her breast. The silhouette becomes more and more clear. It is Jakub Perlman, the eldest son of Aunt Mania, who was taken to Skarzysko. Ania's heart comes back to its place.

'Remember, Ania?' Mum whispers. 'Jakub used to come to visit us on Sundays, the day he did not work, and he would play chess with Father. Remember? Dr Weichert* helped save his two children. His boy is hidden with a Polish family, somewhere in a village, in the sticks, and his daughter is on her own, somewhere in the free world.'

Jakub does not worry about them. They do not kill little children in the free world. He is more worried about Aunt Mania who was taken to Skarzysko and about Renia who was deported to Oswiecim the day before. 'I have some soup left,' Jakub says. 'I have no-one to give it to ... It's for you ... ' He gives them the dish with soup and disappears and they go on walking.

It is dark.

Scene four:

Ania cannot see anything any more, she cannot hear, she has a high temperature and everything that is happening around her must be hallucinations. They are pulling her from all sides, and running alongside her in a great hurry, in a great crowd. *You have to, you have to, Ania, you cannot stop, you cannot fall down, you have to keep up.* It must be Mum holding her up

---

* Dr Michal Weichert was a founder, artistic director and a director of the Youth Theatre in pre-war Poland. During the occupation he was the leader of *Samopomoc Spoleczna* in the Cracow Ghetto, which had been set up as an aid organization for show and was receiving aid from Switzerland. After the war he settled with his family in Israel.

all the time. Ania cannot see a thing but she is trying to keep up in this marathon race, making the last effort.

'Where are we hurrying to so much?' she would like to ask someone. 'Has the war ended?' *Yes, yes, the war is ending. The Russians are close, a bit more, you have to, you have to . . .*

They were locked in a freight car marked 'Auschwitz'.

It is completely dark around, you cannot see a thing, you cannot move, screams and cries blend together into one great lamentation. Reli faints inside the carriage. *They are going to throw her out, they are throwing the dead out of the train, but she is still alive, she is alive, they already want to take her place. She is not, she is alive!* Reli opens her eyes for a moment. It is pitch black. *How long?* At the station they get out of the cars to relieve themselves, the train is sprinkled with lime. *Drink, drink, water, water!* There is no water. They are licking one another's moist bodies. They have to run again. Mum and Ania are dragging Reli, who is fainting now and again.

'Why are you not trying to escape? There are only a few Germans,' somebody says.

Mum points at Reli: 'How?'

The doors of the car shut. It is ghastly. *When is this journey going to be over?* Somebody at the bottom, crushed under a layer of bodies, speaks in a creaking voice. From what she is saying we can understand that our train – a ghost train – is going round and round although we could have reached our destination a long time ago because Auschwitz is not far. But Auschwitz is overcrowded because they are sending many transports of Jews there from the whole of Europe. But there is something happening to these transports so that they still have place for the new ones . . . Ania does not understand anything. It is a hellish journey. Somebody is treading on her head. One of her legs is entangled in somebody else's body. *Never before had it been so frightening . . . never had it been so dark.*

Chapter Eight

The train stopped.

Today I know that it was October, probably one of the last few days of October 1944. Years ago.

Then I thought that the journey from Plaszow to Oswiecim had taken ages.

The huge, towering stalk of the chimney, like a skyscraper, and the smoke gushing out of it, thick and pitch black, and the black and grey, smoking sky, and the large, so-malicious sentence 'Arbeit macht frei', and Mum with a puzzled and frightened look on her face, and Reli, hardly able to stand alone, and the deadly silence of the women getting off the train, and the freezing cold and the desperate helplessness – that is what remained in Ania's memory of her first meeting with Auschwitz-Birkenau.

They were herded, like cattle, into some small building. They were passing by a small window. On the other side of the window pane...Wuska Liebeskind, the wife of Dolek, the hero of the Cracow Ghetto. She was wearing a striped camp shirt, her head clean-shaven, making her beautiful features only more distinguished.

*It would be really important to talk to Wuska. She had disappeared from the Ghetto right after the heroic attack of the youngsters on the 'Cyganeria' café. Does it mean that since then...? That is, here...*Seeing her brought some hope into their hearts. *It would be important to ask her what...why this smoke...?*

Go on, go on, faster, faster, gyorsan, gyorsan . . . incomprehensible words. Hungarian and Slovak mixing with Polish and German. All the time you need to hurry. After that Ania never saw Wuska again; she did not manage to hear one word from her.

They were pushed into a barrack, several dozen women, and the best places were soon taken. The room was much smaller than the large barrack in Plaszow. Mum, Reli and Ania took the berth which looked like a separate bed . . . They were not flanked by the sea of bodies, as in Plaszow . . . These conditions, as if a little bit better than in Plaszow, gave Mum a boost of confidence and energy. She turned into a lioness, put up a fight. She managed to 'organize' two blankets and was moving them around, here and there, in their new 'apartment'. And already, before they managed to rest their weary bones after that dreadful journey lasting for so many hours, they were being rushed again. Young girls in shiny boots, with crops in their hands, shouted in Hungarian: *gyorsan* (faster) and *csend* (quiet).

'They shout in Hungarian, but they are really from Slovakia,' someone explained. 'Jewish. They have been here a long time. They've got posts.'

Ania was curious about who those girls really were and what was going on there. When would they finally give them something to eat? And to drink? Her lips were dry, her stomach empty like a gigantic hole. You could think of nothing else . . . Your intestines twitched, pulsating painfully. 'The next day, you will get your daily food portion the next morning . . . ' The huge chimney never ceased to spit out the thick black smoke. The night came. You could not fall asleep. The hunger would not let you. Hunger dominated the body, the senses, won against tiredness and sleep. The hunger played with your intestines and your nerves. *Before the war people would say they were starving to death. True, you can starve to death. You die slowly and in pain.*

Mum, Reli and Ania were queueing in a large room and

waiting. On the floor next to them were heaps of clothes – dresses, skirts, sweaters, blouses, hats and coats. In good condition; some of them even elegant. *Whose?*

It was easy to guess that the owners of those clothes, some elegant ladies, had put on their best clothes when going on a journey. Now all their garments were lying scattered here. *And how about them?*

Whose things are these?

'Strip naked.' A command is given. 'Faster, faster, faster! Do not mix your lousy rags with what the Dutch women left,' yells the vulgar *Kapo.*

'The Dutch women?'

'Yes, the Jewesses from Holland. Do not ask questions.'

Faster, faster! Their lousy clothes have already disappeared, swept away by the *Kapo* with a large brush, or something that looked like that. With one energetic movement she has swept away all their belongings. *The end of Mum's green dress, the end of anything they had on. They are standing now, barefoot and naked. Like the day they were born, like the day . . . Ania shivers with cold, ashamed of her skinny body. To be born only to live to this? It would have been better not to be born at all. Luckily she still has her family. Mum and Reli are her invisible partition dividing her from the terrible reality, her wall, her support. Nothing is more important than to be together, not to get lost.*

At the end of the barrack they are tattooing numbers. The queue begins to move on, it goes quickly; one by one they reach out their left arms. Somebody comforts them: 'You have no number – you do not exist; you have a number – you will have soup, you will have bread.'

It is Ania's turn. Mum has already been numbered but she hesitates, lingers, even though they are yelling at her and rushing her. 'We must stay together,' her blue sad eyes are saying. Now a young girl with great concentration and a masterly eye is pinpricking A-26804 on Ania's forearm and filling in each mark with blue ink. It does not hurt more than an injection, lots of injections, one next to another. *It is nothing terrible.* Now they are tattooing Reli. *She hates injections, I hope she won't faint, because if she faints then . . .* Reli has got a number too.

The next step is selection.

But then in all probability the first selection had taken place at the beginning, before they tattooed the numbers.

They rush them; all the time they rush them. They make them run naked, their feet in clogs which they keep losing when running. Somewhere, at some point, at some gate there are the Germans, counting, looking at the merchandise. They are in their uniforms, buttoned from top to bottom, scrutinizing the naked women, some straightening their glasses, other wiping the lenses with handkerchiefs. They stand, legs apart, in shiny boots . . . The naked women pass before them . . . not all of them. Some are taken out of the line – and disappear. You cannot see them anywhere afterwards.

Mum, Reli and Ania pass. They have survived their first selection.

'It's not the end,' somebody explains, 'selections happen almost every day here.'

Now they are rushed somewhere else. Faster, faster, into the bath, into the showers. *Are they really going to take a bath?*

'And why not?'

'Because instead of water they let the gas in . . .'

'Those who say that are insane.'

'They are not insane. You *still* do not believe?'

'Go on, go on, faster, faster. It is true, it is all true.'

'Instead of water they let the gas in and they burn the dead bodies in the crematorium.'

'There is a special *Kommando* working there – the *Sonder-kommando*. Some people are forced to work there; some volunteer.'

On the way to the showers each of them is given a small bar of soap. On the soap the letters *RJF*. Someone translates: *Reine Judische Fett* (made fom Jewish fat).

Is that possible? Ania's senses are blunt. She would like to rebel, to scream, scratch, beat, kill. But she is overwhelmed by complete weakness, total powerlessness, her skinny legs walk on their own, like clockwork automata, run in the line – to the bath.

The water is coming from above. The soap does not lather, the water is at first scalding and then cold again.

How skinny I am, Ania suddenly thinks in dread. *My body is not a girl's body. It's a skeleton. A corpse.* Ania-skeleton dissolves in the infinite helplessness. A vortex in her head. *And Mummy? And Reli? It is not them. They are skeletons. We will not make it through the next selection...What soap is that? God Almighty, God Almighty! What sort of soap is that? Who made it? Who took care to have RJF written on top of it? Who? Merchants? Manufacturers?*

The bath is over. Ania wants to get rid of that soap. She has nothing else and that soap she does not want. They leave the room wet. They put on some people's clothes which are thrown at them at the exit: clothes are in abundance here. A few pairs of shoes in all sizes have also been thrown in their direction. The clever ones have got hold of those. There have not been enough for everyone. They are being rushed on with whips. 'Faster, faster, enough of this modelling.' The next transport is waiting. The Germans are standing in a lane, watching them. They are talking to one another, smiling, calling each other 'Herr' and observing other courtesies.

What mothers gave birth to them?

A scrawny girl, perhaps twelve years old, runs past them, cowering from the Germans. *Has she sneaked out of the gas chamber?*...She is looking for her mother...There is no mother. Ania catches the terrified look in her eyes. Somebody pushes her; the little girl disappears.

Suddenly Ania sees familiar faces: Mrs Borstein and one of her three daughters. You would always see the four of them together; now there are only two. Naked, with clean-shaven heads. Most of the women have shaven heads.

'It is too much work,' a skeleton-lady with hair on her head says to Ania, 'they have not managed to shave all of us yet.'

The older Mrs Borstein has sagging breasts, her daughter

walks in such as way as to make the Germans look at her
young body rather than at the sagging breasts of her mother.
Ania's eyes catch the look of the older Mrs B. Ania will never
forget that look.

At the next selection they both went – the mother and the
daughter – to the gas.

Auschwitz-Birkenau. Another Planet. Today people know
more about it than Ania did then, being there.

Today, the researchers of the Oven Age (A. Rudnicki) argue
with Jehiel Dinur (code name: Ka-Tzetnik, number 135633),
who was the first one to use the term 'Another Planet'. Not
'another' because it is ours; it all happened on this very planet.
Educated people with academic degrees planned genocide on
a grand scale, with the use of means calculated in offices and
laboratories. There were many volunteers to execute the plan,
in many fields. And it all happened in the heart of civilization;
at a distance of a few kilometres from the area inhabited by
ordinary people.

And still it was Another Planet.

And no words can convey this today.

At one selection, Renia, the daughter of the God-fearing Aunt
Mania – herself deeply religious – did not make it. She was
pushed onto the other side, with hundreds of others – and
Renia, just like them, disappeared for ever. A day earlier,
when their groups had met, each being rushed in another
direction, Renia had thrown a pair of knickers to Ania. Ania
had not managed to thank her... They had not had time to
exchange even one word. Renia's knickers, good and warm,
were something concrete. They warmed up Ania's half-frozen
body and her sore, hungry-for-love heart. She lost them at the
next bath. Once again she was left with nothing. Perhaps
Renia's knickers will be of use to someone else...

There is no Renia any more. Renia was taken to the gas.

Ania did not have time to say thank you.

*

And still new transports are coming to the camp. In the transports – gypsies and Jews from Greece. The latter are dying like flies.

Banished from sunny Greece, from the Mediterranean Sea, whole families of Greek Jews die of cold and hunger before they reach the crematorium. It is the Polish climate, the Polish winter, that kills them.

The news reaches Ania on her berth, when, thinking of a loaf of fresh bread, she cannot sleep. When she is slowly dying...

The women say we are in Birkenau. This is not even the camp; it is a halfway station to death or to other camps. The real camp is over there. Auschwitz. The place for political prisoners, priests, communists, Poles and Jews. Ania is thinking of the professors from Cracow and of Wuska Liebeskind. *She must be there.*

'There,' an unknown woman from the berth beside her is saying, 'there is a hospital there where they experiment on men, women, children... They let one woman give birth and then tied up her breasts in such a way as to prevent her from breast-feeding. The poor baby was crying before its mother's eyes, begging for food and the poor woman was writhing in pain, her breasts full of milk. There you have it, an experiment – German scientists must know how long a Jewish baby can live under conditions like those... [Rut Elias]. And there are many other, even more cruel experiments. The selections are conducted by a doctor... A doctor... They have an orchestra and "Canada"* and the *Sonderkommando* there, and the prisoners who planned to rebel and escape, and...'

All the Jews are gassed and burnt.

'They burn the gypsies as well, just like the Jews,' another woman informs them.

---

* 'Canada' – warehouses in Auschwitz where things which remained after the Jews were gassed were sorted, put in order, and prepared to be sent to Germany. The prisoners working there were thought to be privileged because they had greater access to valuable goods – such as food, clothes or gold – with which they could sometimes bribe the Germans and win their favours.

Mum divides a slice of bread into three. You can see she is dying of hunger. She is suffering a lot. And Dad asked Ania to take care of her. *How is it possible to take care of her? How to protect her from all this? How much willpower has she had to have to share this bread with us? How much love?!*

Ania misses Father. *Where is he now? Are they tormenting him as well? Mauthausen: what sort of camp is that?*

Is the war ever going to end?

'What is happening here has nothing to do with the war.'

Nobody reacts to these words, nobody has any strength left for philosophy.

The Russians are going west. They have already liberated Cracow...

If we were in Cracow, would we have come back home, to our cosy flat? Who lives there now, in the flat where Ania loved every nook and cranny, every item – and the view from its windows? The beautiful garden of the monastery – is the lilac going to bloom this spring? Does whoever lives in our flat wonder sometimes what has become of us?

Stifled voices and whispers reach the tired brain of Ania: 'There are huge transports of Hungarian Jews flowing into Auschwitz-Birkenau. They started with Hungarian Jews at the very last moment...'

'This war is never going to end.'

Hanan Akavia, at that time Leopold Jacobovits, arrived at Oswiecim in 1944, with one of the transports of Hungarian Jews. He was 17 then and a number: A-5741. His journey from home to the camp was similar to the one remembered by Ania, and the one described in the first book by Eli Wiesel – *Night*. Until the deportation the Wiesel and Jacobovits families lived in the same Rumanian-Hungarian-Jewish town of Sighet – and they came to Oswiecim in the same transport.

Perhaps Ania saw them then, there?

Perhaps she caught Leopold's eye once in passing? They did not know each other then. They were but the anonymous mass; numbers.

Transports move on. It is snowing, the snow is sticking to the clogs, you cannot keep your balance in those clogs. Whoever loses balance, they shoot him. You are lucky if you die at the first shot. Transports move on, here and there, passing one another. Sometimes you can catch someone's eye, find in the frightened, tired eyes a spark of human sensibility, understand the words not spoken, feel the magnetic strength of mutual liking, shared desires.

Most of these people disappear for ever.

Black smoke rises from the huge stalk of the chimney.

Here is a large family: the two brothers Jacobovits who, not such a long time before, used to do sound business together, are here now with their families, at the gates of the crematorium. Young Leopold, called Lipi for short, is a son of one of the respectable Jakobovits brothers. Lipi has got a mother, father, a brother and two sisters. His elder sister Cyli, renowned for her cheerfulness and unusual beauty, has already got a husband and two little children of her own, a son and a daughter.

The other brother's family is even larger; there is also their grandfather and grandmother.

After the selection Lipi is left alone.

Leopold-Hanan lost in Auschwitz his mother, father, brother, sister, grandparents, uncles, cousins and his little niece and nephew. He was left alone, with a handicap and a longing for the rest of his life.

After the war he found out that apart from him only one of his sisters, Cyli (the cheerful one), and her husband, survived Auschwitz. Their children were snatched away from them...

Cyli lives in grief and longing, with a feeling of guilt. She has two post-war children. In between her and her children there is Auschwitz. Her new children do not know how to deal with her; she has never ceased to be there, with those children, the whole family, in front of the chimney of the gigantic oven. She does not want to, she cannot, enjoy anything.

'Our mother is a masochist,' her new children say. They want to understand her but they cannot.

Their mother does not answer. She cannot. She wants to shelter her new children. She does not want to poison their lives. The children, on the other hand, do not ask questions, they try to live normal lives. But how?

'If childhood is the most important period of man's life then our mother had a more normal childhood than we do. She had grandparents, a large family and a cheerful home. We do not have any of that.' The children pity their mother and themselves. They do not ask questions.

Cyli is one of many, although not all of them react in the same way. But it is still impossible to understand what was *Sho'ah*, what happened there, and you cannot understand those who survived.

The Budy *Kommando* would leave Birkenau each day. After the roll-call and the 'breakfast' – each morning a liquid called coffee, and in addition, twice a week, a few grams of bread (the bread they would eat all at once, only Mother would sometimes save a slice 'for the next day'), a slice of sausage (horse meat?) and a spoonful of marmalade – the Budy *Kommando* would stand in line. They were watched over by a *Kapo*, a cross-eyed red-nosed German, who in Oswiecim – the place of mass murder – was doing time for a single homicide. In Ania's eyes that vulgar German, waving her whip in the air all the time, who had killed only one person, was the embodiment of Justice. She could have whipped them, she could have torn their nails off, gouged out their eyes, tormented them at her leisure – and yet she did not do that. She would only rush them to march for a few kilometres, up to the clearing in the woods where, under her supervision, they would saw the trees and carry large trunks, together with the branches, from place to place.

The work was hard and seemed unnecessary. Just one more way of torturing the defenceless victims, who did not have any strength left in them. Within one month they were all turned into 'Muslims';* skin and bones, and sunken eyes, they were dropping on their feet, they did not fight for anything. The cold wind was piercing their almost naked bodies. There were no newspapers or pieces of cloth which you could use to protect your hands and feet from frostbite. Many women could no longer feel their frost-bitten fingers; some were even losing them. Most of them suffered from continuous diarrhoea, defecating foetid greenish liquids – their last bodily juices.

The question was asked: 'Why were we not trying to escape? Our German *Kapo* would not be able to do anything if all of us were to make a run for it. Or, if we decided on the order and began running off one by one, one after another. Why were we not running away?'

It was not fear dictating the lack of initiative and inertia. Those who tried to escape were shot at, but nobody was afraid of losing life. Such life. The much worse fear was that of the reaction of the people in the area. Even if we manage to escape, which door should we knock at? Who is going to let us in, in such a state?

Ania does not believe there are still good people in this world. *If there were they would not allow all this to happen. They would come here to the camp, in masses, to help us, to save us.*

'You are so naive, Ania. Nobody cares for us.'

It is frightening to think that. If it is so then why fight? Why survive?

Nobody is afraid of death. Let them shoot. But her feet do not carry her any more. Mum and Reli are even weaker. *They will not manage to escape.* An incredible tiredness and weakness rule the body and senses. The black cloud of smoke from the crematorium covers the sky above the clearing.

---

* 'Muslims' was the name given to those prisoners who were almost completely physically and mentally exhausted. Adult 'Muslims' weighed only 20-odd kilos. They were frightening to look at because, apart from their excessive thinness, they also exhibited other symptoms – for example, swellings, a change in skin-colouring, problems with speech and breathing, lower bodily temperature, lack of responsiveness to external stimuli, etc. A group of such prisoners seen from afar reminded one of the praying Arabs, hence the popular term.

Once Ania did hear the drone of planes. Huge bombers cut the air, piercing the smoke over Oswiecim, emerging from it in all their might. Suddenly they plunged down and flew roaring right over their heads.

Ania remembered 1939. They were in their flat then, in Cracow. The drone of planes, just like these ones, had brought them all to the Venetian window in the bedroom. Looking up, Izio said: 'Those are German bombers. I saw the swastika on their wings!'

'You must be wrong,' Mum said, trying to relax them. 'Those must be the Polish Army manoeuvres.'

Izio was not wrong. Those were the German planes which then dropped bombs on the innocent streets of Cracow. That was the beginning.

How many years have passed since? A hundred? Two hundred?

It was then that the war broke out. *But to tell the truth, all that burning of the Jews ... did it really begin then, or had it been much earlier?* Izio would often tell her about Amalek* and Haman,** about the Pharaoh† and the Inquisition‡ ... And that even in our prayers we would say and repeat:

---

*   Amalek was a member of the ancient nation of Amalekites, the nomads who attacked the Israelites on their way to the Promised Land during the Exodus. Amalek became the symbol of the eternal enemy of Israel, who in vain attempts to destroy every generation.

** Haman was a minister to the Persian king Ahasuerus, who gave the order to murder all the Jews. This genocide was avoided thanks to Queen Esther, a Jew. To commemorate that event the Jews celebrate Purim, during which they read from the Book of Esther, telling of the story of the beautiful Esther, chosen by the Persian king – who did not know of her Jewish origins – for his wife. Esther made the king sentence Haman, and other enemies of the Jews, to death.

†   Pharaoh was the title of Egyptian kings in Biblical times. Here, the ruler of Egypt, during the Exodus of the Israelites set free by him. The fast multiplying of the Jews in slavery frightened the Egyptians; which is why he decided to put an end to it by force. God had not forsaken His people and gave them Moses, the saviour, and the opposition of the Pharaoh was broken by means of the miracles known as the plagues.

‡   The Inquisition was a political-judicial institution of the Catholic Church, directed against all the movements which had been proclaimed heretical, especially in Spain and Portugal. Called to life in Spain in 1215, it remained active until 1835. From the end of the thirteenth century it became especially interested in the Jews, particularly those who had converted to Catholicism [Marranos]. Some Jews pretended to convert to save their lives, others fled Spain and Portugal and scattered across Europe. The Inquisition was responsible for the death of many thousands of victims.

In every generation they want to destroy us
And the Lord, may his name be praised,
Delivers us from their hands.

Izio knew. He knew History – the ancient and the new...
But does God deliver us? And why in every generation? Why?
Why us?

Even under those terrible conditions, hungry and cold, doing Sisyphean work, you cannot stop thinking.

Ania lifts her head, she wants to see whose planes are circling above Oswiecim. If Izio were here, he would know in an instant they were not German. Perhaps he would say: 'Here the cycle comes to an end. The war is ending.'

But Izio is not here. It is a pity that he did not make it.

Now Ania can see clearly: those are American planes. If Izio were here, he would say they could have come a long time before, they could have bombed Auschwitz ages before.

They can still bomb the crematorium now, its huge chimney, and those inhuman baths, and this whole hideous, awful death factory. If they cannot aim precisely, let them drop their bombs wherever they can. On the crematorium and on us, we do not care, we have no more strength anyway...

Ania reaches out to the planes, begging, imploring...

Other women, just like her, are running on their thin legs after the planes, reaching out, begging, imploring.

In vain.

American planes, their last grain of hope, disappear, fly away. They slowly rise in the air and disappear, leaving Ania and her companions to their evil fate in this Auschwitz-Birkenau-Budy, with the German criminal and everything that is happening around.

Heaven is not fair for everyone. On the front lines, not far away, where the armies fight, that terrible war is coming to an end. It is already clear that the Nazi beast will be defeated. But here, on this planet, where they are torturing defenceless people, the nightmare continues.

There is no heaven above Oswiecim.

The blue sky is covered in black smoke.

No help from anywhere.

Birds circle over the clearing, rising slowly and going farther and farther from that cursed, miserable land, soaked in the blood and covered with the ashes of millions of innocent people.

The criminal-*Kapo* leads a column of women who can barely walk back to Birkenau. There they are awaited by other criminals with their whips and curses.

Even today black ravens circle over the site of genocide.

Excursions come and go – and nobody understands.

Chapter Nine*

Uncle Arthur opened the door. Aunt Mala was standing behind him scrutinizing the newly arrived, her eyes open wide. A few minutes passed in silence. Suddenly Aunt Mala exclaimed: 'Margot! But it's Margot...'**

Uncle Arthur reached out his hand, broad, strong, similar to Father's, and exclaimed in embarrassment: 'Margot! Dear Margot.'

They led her into the room. Zygi was not at home. The room was engulfed in cool darkness. Uncle Arthur raised the blinds and opened the window. The humid heat of Tel Aviv *khamsin* invaded the room. In the evening light Margot noticed modest furniture with faded covers. An antique silver sugar bowl stood on a little table in the corner, the only valuable item from another world. Margot stopped, embarrassed and pensive, in the middle of the room, staring at the silver bowl. A layer of patina seemed to melt under her stare and the bowl seemed to speak to her in mysterious words...

'What's going on, Margot?' asked Uncle Arthur. 'Come, sit down and tell us.'

Margot looked at him, a silent question in her eyes. *What shall I tell you? I know you would like to hear everything but... I can't, I don't know where to start.*

She sat there miserable, unable to gather her thoughts. Uncle Arthur and Aunt Mala exchanged worried glances.

---

* This has been previously published as 'Margot's Silver Sugar Bowl'.
** Margot is Ania.

'Try, Margot, try to remember,' said her aunt and her uncle added: 'Each one of us has been through something and we need to tell others about it. I have so many things to tell you myself.'

'I have not forgotten and I shall never forget.'

They approached her both, ready to listen. And she just shrank in her pain and kept silent.

Margot was ten and her sister, Rut, twelve. Everybody around them was shocked and appalled by the war which had broken out so suddenly and invaded their apparent Paradise. The Polish Army, the fame and might of which was a subject of many a history lesson at school, was defeated. The Germans marched into the town, not hiding their murderous intentions.

On the third day after the taking of the city, parents went out to talk to their friends and to decide how to get out of their predicament. 'We must go out but we will try to be back soon. Lock the door and don't answer it to anyone. Anyone.'

After their parents had gone Rut locked the door, turning the key twice in the lock, and had switched off the lights, leaving only a bedside light on, and drawn the curtains. They were not afraid at the beginning. They both took their shoes off, sat cross-legged on the bed and started to play draughts. They were surrounded by absolute silence. However, in time, they began to feel uneasy, their anxiety growing with each minute. They began to talk in low voices; then only to whisper. They got bored with draughts. Rut tiptoed to the drawer in their parents' room and fetched the family album with photographs.

Suddenly – a doorbell. The girls jumped. They huddled closely to each other and sat quietly holding their breaths. The bell rang again, and then again and again... And, in between the ringing, knocking on the door. The ringing and knocking, more and more persistent, ran through the children like an electric current. But nobody was yelling or kicking at the door. The girls sat frightened, white as sheets. Margot got stomach ache.

'Maybe we should open? I must go to the toi...,' she cried quietly.

'Who could that be?' whispered Rut, and Margot understood that her sister also did not believe that the person behind the door was evil, or a criminal.

'Maybe it's one of the neighbours?' Margot said, all shrivelled in pain... 'But we were told not to open the door, and I once heard our parents say they did not trust the neighbours either.'

Rut closed Margot's mouth with one hand and she stroked her hair with another. Again someone rang the bell and knocked, and then there were more alternate rings and knocks. In the end everything went quiet, and the children's ears pricked at the noise of footsteps fading away in the distance.

Everything went silent. But even before Margot managed to make it to the bathroom they heard the whiz of the bullet right beneath their window followed by shouting in German. Rut squeezed Margot's hand and the eyes of both girls widened in fear. They could not tell how long it all lasted. The street and the house were all quiet but they still could not move out of fear.

When their parents came back Margot burst into tears. It was not the usual pre-war crying. Margot was unable to control the short stifled sobs escaping her breast.

'Calm down, Margot,' Daddy asked.

His face was all worry and Margot's little heart ached even more. *As if it were not enough that Father has so many serious problems, here I am adding some more*, she thought sadly.

Mummy stroked her hair and kissed her. 'You did well not to open the door. These days you cannot let strangers into the house...'

'Who could it have been?' asked Rut.

Nobody answered her.

'There were searches and round-ups,' Mother said. 'The Germans, and together with them some local scum, were pulling Jews out of their houses, making them face the wall. They were plundering and vandalizing their flats. Who knows what is ahead of us? God . . . If only we could get out of here . . . If only there was a way . . . We were lucky to get back home.'

'That man who was knocking on our door, he wasn't German,' Rut persisted. 'Who could it have been?'

'It doesn't matter, children . . . You were right not to have answered,' Mother said and tucked in Margot, who was already in her bed. 'Rut, you go to bed as well . . . You've had enough excitement for today.'

'He was not German,' Rut repeated, lost in thought.

Margot looked up and mumbled something incomprehensible. *Her uncle and aunt are waiting but how to tell them even about that one evening? How to convey the feeling of fear overwhelming them for that one brief hour, preceding dozens of thousands of other hours of fear and dread?*

In the meantime Aunt Mala brought a tray of fruit, soda water, raspberry juice, glasses and plates. Uncle Arthur made himself comfortable in his armchair and only Margot sat motionless like a stone.

'Do you remember, Margot, that I came to Poland in the summer of 1939?' started Uncle Arthur. 'I came alone, for a short break. I had a few things to settle because, even though we had already been for four years in Eretz-Israel, I still had many friends in Poland, whom I wanted to see and, first of all, you – my close family. The outbreak of war found me in Poland. You should remember, Margot, that overwhelming panic that came over everyone, and the Jews in particular. You should remember what it felt like in the city then. All the roads of escape cut off.

'As a Mandate citizen* I had a British passport. I knew I had to be gone as quickly as possible. British citizens had to go to the Gestapo offices to receive a pass enabling them to

---

* Between 1920 and 1948 Great Britain held a Mandate over Palestine, given to it by the League of Nations.

leave. I do not want to get into details now... I just want you to know, Margot, that miraculously – thanks to a moment of confusion and misunderstanding I had taken advantage of – I managed to get the passes for the four of you as well... I ran out of the Gestapo office holding the precious papers in my hands and trembling in fear that one of those criminals could come after me, snatch them out of my hands and render them null and void. I ran like crazy, not being able to believe myself what I had just done... I knew that the trains had ceased to operate regularly and checked when we had the train towards the border the next day... I also knew I had to reach you before the curfew to let you know that we had to leave Poland together the next morning.

'So here I am dashing through the streets, my heart pounding. I am crying and laughing at the same time. I want to be with you so badly, to tell you what I have done, help you pack... I hope we will make it... All the way I was convincing myself that we were going to make it because my passport was real just as the Gestapo passes were real... When Mala, Zygi and myself had been leaving Poland before the war, your father had not wanted to go. "We feel all right here," he used to say. He had not listened to me when I told him that things were getting out of control. But I knew that at that point you were going to accept my suggestion and that you were going to leave with me. So here I am running to see you... I can hear the Germans yelling and shooting in other streets – certainly not in the air. I did not pay attention and kept on running. Finally I made it to the gate of your house. I ran upstairs three steps at a time and rang the bell. I was covered in cold sweat when I understood that there was nobody in the flat. In desperation I rang and knocked, knocked and rang, but the doors did not open. I cried...'

Margot, all the time pale and overcome with fear, stifled a cry and cowered like a wounded animal.

'The German yelling was getting louder and I could hear their loud footsteps approaching the house where I was standing in front of your door,' Uncle Arthur continued. 'I thought if I stayed a little longer I might not leave myself...I thought about Mali and Zygi waiting for my return...The next morning I left Poland and I never heard of you again.'

Uncle Arthur finished his story and looked at Margot. She sat there motionless, petrified.

'We were at home when you knocked on the door, Uncle,' she said tentatively. 'We heard you knocking...'

The plate with grapes Aunt Mala was holding in her hands dropped onto the floor, breaking into pieces.

'Margot!!!'

How much judgement, how many accusations were in this one exclamation of Aunt Mala!

'Margot!!' Uncle Arthur rose from his armchair. 'What did you say? You were at home then? Why on earth did you not open the bloody door?!' Suddenly he raised his voice: 'Why the hell didn't you open?'

Margot was silent. They went silent themselves, exchanging glances. She found it difficult to stand. Her uncle and aunt suddenly began to disappear in the distance, growing smaller and smaller, more and more distant...And from the corner of the room suddenly the old sugar bowl emerged, growing larger and larger, closer and closer.

Somebody turned the key in the main door. Margot started. *Is that Zygi?* A young male voice reached her from the hall: 'What's happening? Are you all asleep? I'm in a great hurry, I've got a meeting at six.'

'Just a minute,' said Aunt Mala and went into the hall.

Margot got up but Uncle Arthur stopped her and said: 'He's in a hurry.'

Margot sat down again. Suddenly she felt the well-known taste of humiliation. *Zygi is in a hurry? Zygi has no time? How about her? How about her time? Her time does not exist. It has frozen. There is no future for her because her past is no past. It does not fit into the framework of any human idea. Nobody is able to understand it. And this macabre time lives only in her...But some other memories live in her too. What happened some time ago . . . Something did happen . . . How and when?*

Somewhere in a beautiful holiday resort in the Tatra mountains Margot's parents rented a little cottage for the summer. There was a brook not far from the cottage, its crystal-clear water bursting its banks and washing millions of colourful pebbles. A little girl called Margot is standing not far from the stream looking at the strong current. Next to her a boy called Zygi. Zygi is seven. Both have gathered dried sticks and twigs and potatoes, and are going towards the river with their loot.

'We'll make the fire here,' says Zygi, who came with his mother from Eretz-Israel to spend his holidays in Poland because in Palestine it is terribly hot in the summer.

'Look how many trees there are around, the fire might spread,' warned little Margot. 'Our house might get burnt.'

'You're right,' Zygi agreed and found the way out immediately. 'We can light our fire on the island, just like Robinson Crusoe.'

The children took their shoes off, step by step walked over the sharp-edged stones, up to their knees in water. Margot tried not to lose her balance, not to behave like a baby. In this way they reached an islet. The water was pounding on its shores, breaking into thousands of shimmering droplets.

'We're going to make our fire here,' decided little Margot and began to set the sticks and twigs in a pile.

Zygi slowly reached into his pocket and took out a box of matches. A tiny good flame warmed and cheered the little hearts of the children.

That tiny flame had died a long time ago. After that there was only that gigantic fire, raging, consuming, annihilating everything and everyone. Aunt Mala and Zygi had managed to return to Palestine in peace.

Zygi entered the room. Handsome, healthy, sporty. Embarrassed, he hardly even looked her way.

'But it's Margot, your cousin,' said his mother.

'*Shalom*,' said Zygi, and asked, 'Have you got anything to eat?'

Margot felt the blood running to her face.

'I'm in a hurry,' said Zygi and followed his mother into the kitchen.

Uncle Arthur went with them. Passing by Margot, he shrugged his shoulders as if wanting to say 'What can you do?' He said: '*Palmachnik.*'*

She did not understand the word anyway. When she was left alone she looked around her relatives' flat. They had three rooms: the living room they were in, the bedroom and Zygi's room. *There is no room for me here*, she thought.

In the meantime the others returned from the kitchen.

'*Shalom*,' Zygi said again, this time looking at her.

'*Shalom*,' she answered and she did not look at him that time.

When the door closed behind Zygi her uncle asked: 'What are your plans, Margot?'

'Of course, you can stay with us,' said Aunt Mala, glancing at the sofa in the living room.

'I will go to the *kibbutz*,' said Margot tentatively.

She asked herself many times: 'What are your plans, Margot? What are you going to do?' On the boat taking her from Europe to the country the *shaliyah*** asked her the same question. 'What would you like to do, Margot? Have you already decided where you would like to go?'

'Yes,' Margot answered, a little ashamed of herself. 'I know. I would really like to study.'

'No, Margot, you haven't understood me. I wasn't asking about that. I asked if you have decided on your ideology. Which party would you like to join? There are

---

*   *Palmach* were the armed troops of the Haganah (self-defence). This was the Hebrew acronym for Pluggot Machatz, or 'Shock Companies'.

**   *Shaliyah* – literally 'a messenger', colloquially a representative of the Jewish agency.

many. Also *kibbutzim* are divided according to their political opinions.'

'What is he talking about?' Margot wondered. One more time she tried to discuss the possibility of studying but a woman standing next to them on the deck butted in, her voice ironic: 'Study! Study! They have only just come here and they already want to study! We escaped from universities to plough the fields, we preferred to build roads, to drain swamps and these new ones – they have only just come here and they already want to study... The Jewish people have had enough of the professors!'

This is what that rough woman told confused Margot on the deck of the ship, and Margot thought that maybe that strange woman was right and that she, Margot, was a descendant of those great Jewish professors who throughout the centuries had served other nations and – in exchange for their services – were murdered...

'Look how spoilt they are,' the woman continued and someone standing next to her added: 'They all went like lambs to the slaughter.'

'I'll go to a *kibbutz*,' Margot said to the *Sochnut** man, but he was not happy with her declaration and insisted: 'But which *kibbutz*, my child? I told you they were divided according to their political opinions.'

'I'll go wherever they need working hands. I don't care about opinions,' Margot answered, not knowing exactly what he meant.

'You must have political education; you must be more aware,' said the *shaliyah*.

'I have relatives in Tel Aviv,' said Margot.

The representative of *Sochnut* wrote down the name of his *kibbutz* in Galilee for her.

'Take this. Just in case.'

'I will go to the *kibbutz*,' Margot told her aunt and uncle.

---

* *Sochnut* was the Jewish Agency.

'There is no rush, you've got time to think about it,' answered Aunt Mala, and Uncle Arthur added: 'You haven't told us anything, Margot...So far I have been doing all the talking myself. What happened to your parents? Where is Rut? Weren't you together? Tell us.'

A mist covered her eyes and she began to see fragments of pictures emerging from it: dry human bones, a baby – still alive and breathing – tossed onto a pile of dead women's bodies. The dead women have long hair, those who are still breathing are bald. Naked bodies hang in a row, swaying in the wind. Legs in black high boots trod on the bodies of living children. Those in boots are laughing loudly. A dirty toilet bowl next to the head of dying Rut. Margot is holding the bony hand of her sister but this hand is slipping out of hers. Margot wants to scream but no voice escapes her lips. Next to the head of dying Rut a clogged toilet bowl. You cannot...not any more...

'I cannot tell you anything...Maybe some other time,' she said.

Her uncle and aunt exchanged glances.

'I'll get us something to eat,' said Aunt Mala.

'I'll help you,' offered Uncle Arthur and waddled into the kitchen in her footsteps.

'You rest, Margot,' he said

She was left alone in the room. After a while she hesitatingly approached the table with the beautiful silver sugar bowl, picked it up and held it against her hot cheek. The touch felt soothing. Then she put the sugar bowl back in its place, tiptoed to the door herself and opened it quietly.

The Tel Aviv night enveloped her in its hot, stifling breath. The street was full of people, rushing in different directions. Passers-by were passing her by, not noticing. Margot's legs felt as if they were made of lead and her head was heavy and – empty.

'Without God...Is God going to come back?'

Afterword

The book you have in your hands was written in two different periods. The first six chapters and Introduction were written in Hebrew in 1975. It was 30 years after the liberation (every time I write this word I feel an intuitive need to put it in inverted commas). It was my first writing attempt in Hebrew, my first spontaneous explosion of stifled emotions and memories.

On the cover of the first edition of my book the Israeli editor wrote in Hebrew and, which was unusual, in English: '...for 30 years Miriam Akavia held back her natural writing power, and only now she allows herself to put down in writing what she experienced: *Childhood at Fall** – written in three months of fever – is the result.'

An End to Childhood is the result of the feverish putting down on paper of what was held back for 30 years. The story, which exploded out of me within those three months of writing by night, after the days filled up with going out to work and coming home to do the housework and take care of my daughters who were still at home, made me a writer. It stemmed from two main needs: my innate love of writing and my obsessive urge to tell the story.

Having written *An End to Childhood* I knew that I had broken the vow of silence – the rule not imposed by any law although observed in practice. But I felt that I could not stand the silence any longer. The incessant anxiety within me,

---

*   *Childhood at Fall* was also published in English under the titles *The Autumn of Youth* and *An End of Childhood*.

which until then I had been trying to hide and lull in many ways, had brimmed over. After that, further pictures, further stories, have never ceased to emerge from a soul pregnant with memories. They have been pouring out onto the page, in a sense releasing my troubled soul from its burden.

After *An End to Childhood*, more stories and novels were published, almost all of them constructed from the same 'parts', cut out from the same fabric. 'Margot's Silver Sugar Bowl' can be read as a epilogue and 'My Own Vineyard' as a prologue to *An End to Childhood*. In the final part of *My Vineyard*, Jurek, Reli and Ani a, whom we meet in *Childhood at Fall*, are carefree (even if not so completely) children. Many characters from *My Vineyard* return also in the stories collected in *The Price*.

My Vineyard, together with an array of characters it describes (families of Weinfeld, Plessner, Perlman, Orbach, Herzig, Karmel and Freulich), is a reservoir of all sorts of human problems, emotions, and situations – both interpersonal and Polish–Jewish relations. Such richness is a sure source of inspiration. Finally, it is one of the last pictures of the normal Jewish world in Poland. When I was working on *My Vineyard*, apart from the strong need to write the family chronicle, to save my dearest ones from being forgotten and to distinguish them from the mass of six million, I thought about my Israeli children. About my own children and about the others for whom my Polish past, so intensely alive in me, is beyond reach. My intuition told me to describe pre-war family events, even more so those that had taken place with my beautiful, beloved Cracow in the background, and in this way to bring the young readers closer and prepare them for what was going to happen there later. Those who get to know the world described in *My Vineyard* will find it easier to understand the same world during *Sho'ah*. And even if not then, perhaps at least they will love the characters a little bit and will not pass a harsh judgement on them by saying that they went like lambs to the slaughter.

Going back to the stories from *The Price* – they tell of the real events, of the war life of Irka and her family (mother Hania, father Olek-Tedy, little sister Nina-Dana), of the post-war fate of cousin Meir from Chrzanów and of Ania herself, who reappears once as Margot, once as Dora'le and a few times as a narrator (in 'Nelly' and other stories).

Even reading the Israeli children's novel *Galia and Miklosz: Breaking Up*, which I wrote, it is easy to guess that the mother of young Galia and Wered (both born in Israel) is no one else but Ania from *An End to Childhood*.

And what happened to real Ania after she had come back from Lvov?

Some readers persistently asked me what happened to Jurek and Ania. After the unclear ending of the first version of *An End to Childhood* they wanted to know what really happened to them. Some, aware of the autobiographical threads in most of my books, were trying to read each of them as a possible sequel to *Childhood at Fall*.

The first version of *An End to Childhood* finishes when Izio-Jurek, who stays in Lvov with Aryan papers, falls into the hands of the Gestapo and Miriam-Ania decides to return to the Ghetto in Cracow. Their further story remained untold until today. Today – in 1994, after a 20-year break, 50 years after those tragic events took place – I have written the sequel to continue the story and I can give you the new *An End to Childhood*. I have added three more chapters to the previous version, the final one of which describes laconically, from the point of view of the 16-year-old Ania, their time in Auschwitz-Birkenau in winter 1944/45.

Perhaps even this time the reader will not be satisfied and ask: 'What happened later?'

The war was not officially over for us until April. After Auschwitz-Birkenau there was also a macabre journey, today known as 'The march of death'. There was also the hellish Bergen Belsen – Hell of Hells. There, on the piles of bodies, both dead and those still twitching in agony, the tormented Mother died. The tormented Father ended his life in Mauthausen's stone quarries at the same time.

Why am I not writing about all that and not describing the miserable 'liberation', the sad belated end of the war? I could have written about my physical and mental state, about diseases, about mass deaths after the 'liberation', about the two years spent in hospitals... About the heart so filled with longing that it could not take it... About woe and sorrow; great woe and sorrow: why?

And about the desire for revenge!

And about the pain of homelessness. And about the painful feeling of not belonging...

I cannot write about all that any more. When I wanted to, there were not many people who cared; and today so many things have been written on the subject that my life experience, which I will never allow myself to expand on to include fictitious events, is not going to be attractive, is not going to be anything 'new'.

I hope Henryk Grynberg will excuse me for quoting him, but I believe his words are also mine. Thanks to him I do not feel lonely as a writer and as a survivor. Speaking from my experience those two identities combined in one person are inevitably bound to compete with each other. It may seem that one of them supports the other, but it is not so. When people find out that I was in the Ghetto and in the camps I cease to exist in their minds as a writer. My effort to use literature as a medium, as an instrument to tell the story, which has been the essence of my life, comes a poor second.

And some more Grynberg: '...The texts may be based on facts, but... the language and form, or the children narrative, may be one of the stylistic techniques which enables us to approach that inexpressible experience.'

When speaking of 'the children narrative', Grynberg was thinking of his *Children of Zion*. I can say the same about my *An End to Childhood*.

And one more thought of Grynberg's with which I absolutely agree: '...I do it [write] first of all for myself, but I also speak on behalf of all those who lent me their voices... the survivors have the right to represent the victims...because the people who were dying kept asking: tell the world. This is a message...This is a duty.'

This is the duty I have been trying to fulfil all my life. The new edition of *An End to Childhood* is but one more proof of that.

Miriam Akavia